GRANDMA KNOWS BEST

GREAT CLEANING SECRETS

BY
CHEF TONY NOTARO
&
DR. MYLES H. BADER

YOU WILL NEVER HAVE TO PURCHASE ANOTHER EXPENSIVE CLEANING PRODUCT...

ENVIRO-S
SAVE HUND

D1059417

GRANDMA KNOWS BEST
GREAT CLEANING SECRETS

BY
CHEF TONY NOTARO
&
DR. MYLES H. BADER

Illustrations: Deborah, Randy & Veronica Peek
Cover Design: Al Cavallo & Diana Barbetti

ISBN:978-0-9882955-8-2
Printed and bound in the Unites States

10 9 8 7 6 5 4 3 2

Telebrands Press
79 Two Bridges Road
Fairfield, NJ 07004

www.telebrands.com

Please note: While this compilation of Cleaning Secrets will solve many problems, total success cannot be guaranteed. Neither the authors, publisher, manufacturer, nor distributor can assume responsibility for the effectiveness of the suggestions.

Table Of Contents

A WORD ABOUT DR. BADER

Dr. Myles H. Bader (known as the wizard of food) has been interviewed on over 6,000 radio and television shows in the United States and Canada and is internationally recognized as a leader in the fields of Preventive Care and Wellness. Appearances on television shows include The Oprah Winfrey Show, The Discovery Channel, Crook and Chase, America's Talking, Trinity Broadcasting, QVC, Smart Solutions, Help at Home, Fox & Friends, HGTV, HSN, NBC, etc.

Dr. Bader received his Doctoral Degree from Loma Linda University and is board certified in Preventive Care. He has practiced in the fields of weight control, exercise physiology, stress management, counseled in all areas of nutrition and has lectured extensively on anti-aging for 30 years. During this period he established prevention and executive health programs for numerous safety departments, city governments, and Fortune 500 companies.

Dr. Bader has authored 19 books including 20,001 Kitchen Secrets, Grandmother's Kitchen Wisdom Series, Club the Bugs & Scare the Critters, Cookbook's Companion, 1,001 Secret Money Saving Formulas, 10,001 Food Facts, Chef's Secrets & Household Hints, 5,001 Mysteries of Liquids & Cooking Secrets, 250 Future Food Facts & Predictions for the Millennium, To Supplement or Not to Supplement, and The Wellness Desk Reference. Dr. Bader's books have been sold through Reader's Digest, Doubleday, Book of the Month Club, QVC, HSN and Barnes & Noble.

INTRODUCTION

The average home today contains more chemicals than the average chemical lab of 100 years ago. Consumers have little knowledge of the ingredients in most of the products they use. Many of the product ingredients are potentially hazardous.

The explosion of the chemical age during and after World War II provided us with a bonanza of new products to replace all the simple ingredient products that generations had used for hundreds of years. Along with these chemical products came an increase in a number of chemical-related illnesses that were not as prevalent in our society until then, the worst being cancer.

When many of these new products are used commercially, they are subjected to various health and safety standards; yet the same substances are used freely and in many instances, carelessly, in our homes. As a result, illnesses and injuries occur that may have been prevented if consumers had more knowledge about the products they use and disposed of safely.

Many illnesses that are associated with chemicals found in the home are mainly benign. These symptoms include headaches, nausea, shortness of breath, eye irritation, sore throats and dizziness. However, some products are associated with some of the more serious illness symptoms such as skin rashes, cancer, cardiac problems and respiratory distress.

The products used in this book are all safe products that can be used around the house to clean just about everything you are presently cleaning using commercial products.

The cost of these products is minimal and you probably have every one of them already in your home.

Almost all are environmentally safe and if used as recommended will do an excellent job of cleaning your home at a fraction of the cost of the commercial products you are presently purchasing.

Many commercial products contain chemicals that may leave a residue in the air in the home reducing the air quality. Indoor air pollution is a problem in many homes and the sale of air purifiers in the United States has turned into a big business. Not only do we suffer from these chemicals but many residues from them are released into the environment and have been related to global change and other forms of pollution.

NOTE:
This book has over 1,000 cleaning tips since many of the paragraphs contain more than one tip.

The following information will provide some important insight into some of the toxic chemicals we have around our homes. There are many hazards in common consumer products that we use every day.

THE KITCHEN

These cleaning agents consist of dishwasher detergents, drain cleaners, all-purpose cleaners, ammonia-based cleaners, copper and brass cleaners, silverware cleaners, oven cleaners, glass cleaners, floor polish, furniture polish, chrome cleaner and even some scouring powders.

> - **Chlorine Bleach (sodium hypochlorite):** If you accidentally mix bleach with an ammonia-based product it is capable of releasing toxic chloramines gas. Exposure to this gas can cause respiratory distress and shortness of breath.
> - **Metal Polishes (petroleum distillate base):** If the fumes get into your eyes, it may cause temporary eye clouding; longer exposure may even damage the central nervous system and affect your kidneys, cause skin eruptions, etc.
> - **Disinfectants (phenol & cresol):** These are corrosives and may cause fainting, ataxia, diarrhea, kidney and liver damage.
> - **Glass Cleaner (ammonia):** Ammonia is an eye irritant and can cause headaches and irritate your lungs.
> - **Floor & Furniture Polishes (nitrobenzene):** Can cause skin problems, respiratory distress and nausea. Nitrobenzene has been associated with cancer and birth defects.
> - **Preservative (formaldehyde):** A known carcinogen and capable of forming free radicals in the body; a strong irritant to eyes, nose, throat and lungs.
> - **Abrasive Cleaners:** Trisodium phosphate (TSP).
> - **Household Batteries:** Mercury, zinc, lithium, cadmium.
> - **Dishwashing Liquid:** May contain naphtha (neurotoxin), sodium nitrates and phosphates.

- ➢ **Automatic Dishwasher Detergent:** Phosphates, chlorine, sodium silicates, etc.
- ➢ **Oven Cleaners:** Methylene chloride, lye, ammonia and many other poisons.

THE LAUNDRY ROOM

Most products contain toxic ingredients: detergents, carpet cleaners, mothballs, deodorizers, laundry softeners, mold cleaners, spot removers and silver polish.

- ➢ **Spot Removers & Carpet Cleaners (solvents):** May cause liver and kidney damage if ingested; can cause cancer in lab animals.
- ➢ **Mothballs (paradichlorobenzine or naphthalene):** Possible carcinogen that may cause damage to eyes, liver, kidneys, skin and central nervous system.
- ➢ **Toilet Cleaner (hydrochloric acid or sodium acid sulfate):** Can cause skin burn, nausea, diarrhea, and may be fatal if ingested. Has been known to cause blindness if splashed in eyes.
- ➢ **Drain Cleaners:** Deadly poisons. May contain lye, bleach, ammonia, HCL and sulfuric acid.
- ➢ **Fabric Softener (residues and fragrances):** May be irritating to susceptible individuals.
- ➢ **Spray Starch (different from non-aerosols and may include formaldehyde or phenols):** Aerosols can irritate lungs.
- ➢ **Flea Collars (carbamates, pyrethins, organophosphates):** Can cause cancer in lab animals and are free radical producers.
- ➢ **Roach & Ant Killers (pyrethins):** Free radical producers and skin irritants.
- ➢ **Rat Poison (warfarin & strychnine):** Deadly poisons to all living creatures.

THE LIVING ROOM AND BEDROOM

Many items in a typical American home can be harmful. If a fabric is labeled "wrinkle-resistant" it may have been treated with formaldehyde resin. Wrinkle-resistant items can include no-iron sheets, sheets, nightgowns, bedding and curtains. If the fabric is labeled "permanent press" or "easy care" there may be a problem.

Pressed wood furniture may contain formaldehyde or other chemicals. Synthetic carpeting is treated with pesticides and fungicides. Many of the office or commercial carpet latex backings are treated with a chemical that has been found to be responsible for "sick" office buildings.

Furniture polishes and cleaners contain mineral spirits, diglycol laurate, petroleum distillates, carbolic acid, nitrobenzene, etc. Nitrobenzene is very toxic and can actually be absorbed through the skin.

THE BATHROOM

There are numerous cosmetics and personal care products that contain hazardous chemical ingredients.

> - **Shampoos (formaldehyde, cresol, nitrates, glycols and sulfur compounds):** nitrates can convert in the body to a carcinogen called a nitrosamine. The other chemicals may increase free radical production.
> - **Hairspray (propellants, formaldehyde resins):** aerosols can damage the environment and formaldehyde may cause cancerous tumors in lab animals.
> - **Deodorants & Antiperspirants (aerosol propellants, formaldehyde, aluminum chlorhydrate, ammonia):** all have been implicated in either cancerous tumor Sin lab animals or in free radical production.
> - **Lotions, Creams & Moisturizers (phenol, cresol):** free radical producers.
> - **Toilet Cleaners:** oxalic acid.

THE ARTS & CRAFT ROOM

Recent legislation is now controlling many chemicals that have been used in hobbies and model building; however, there are still many that have risk factors. These dangerous chemicals and metals include:

> **Lead:** found in stained glass materials, ceramic glazes and pigments.
> **Cadmium:** found in silver solders, ceramic glazes, fluxes and pigments.
> **Chromium:** found in paint pigments and ceramic colors.
> **Manganese Dioxide:** found in ceramic colors, brown oil and acrylic paint pigments.
> **Cobalt:** found in acrylic paint pigments and blue oil.
> **Formaldehyde:** used as a preservative in most acrylic paints and photographic supplies.
> **Aromatic Hydrocarbons:** found in paints and varnish removers, permanent markers, aerosol sprays, etc.
> **Chlorinated Hydrocarbons (solvents):** found in varnish, ink, rubber cement, paint removers, aerosol sprays.
> **Petroleum Distillates (solvents):** found in paint and rubber cement thinners, spray adhesives, silk-screen inks, etc.
> **Glycol Ethers & Acetates:** found in photographic products, lacquer thinners, paints, aerosol sprays, etc.

THE GARAGE

An abundance of products found in almost every garage are hazardous to your health. These include paint thinners, paints, gasoline, kerosene, glues, benzene, mineral spirits, turpentine, motor oils, lubricating oils, etc.

> **Chlorinated Aliphatic & Aromatic Hydrocarbons:** found in paint thinners; studies have found that they can cause liver and kidney damage with overexposure over long periods of time.
> **Petroleum Hydrocarbons & Heavy Metals:** found in gasoline, motor oils, transmission fluids and benzene, which are related to skin and lung cancer.

- ➢ **Mineral Spirits:** found in oil-based paints; a skin, eye, nose, throat and lung, irritant. High concentrations have been related to nervous system damage, unconsciousness and even death.
- ➢ **Ketones:** found in paint thinners and other similar products may cause various types of respiratory distress related to different forms of the chemical.
- ➢ **Sulfuric Acid & Lead:** car batteries.
- ➢ **Glycol Esters & Heavy Metals:** brake fluids.
- ➢ **Toluene:** found in wood putty; very toxic. Causes skin, kidney, liver and central nervous system damage and may damage the reproductive system.
- ➢ **Muriatic Acid, Sodium Hyprochlorite:** found in pool chemicals.
- ➢ **Ethylene Glycol:** found in antifreeze.

THE GARDEN SHED

Here we will find some of the most dangerous chemicals can be found in the garden shed. There are over 1,400 pesticides, herbicides and fungicides that contain harmful ingredients in consumer products. When they combine with other toxic substances such as solvents they pose a risk to our health. Pesticides are present in over 34,000 different product formulations.

- ➢ **House Plant Insecticides:** malathion and methoprene are potent free radical producers.

THE PATIO

Get out the barbecue, but remember that the charcoal lighter fluid contains petroleum distillates that can impart a chemical taste to the foods. Some of these fluids also contain benzene, which is a known human carcinogen and free radical producer.

JUST THE FACTS FOR THE
AVERAGE CITY OF 100,000 POPULATION

170 tons or 340,000 pounds of household cleaners are released into your home drains every year in the average city, as are

4 tons of toilet bowl cleaner;

4 tons of used motor oil products.

$3\frac{1}{2}$ pounds of waste materials (garbage) are contributed by each person every day.

SAFE CLEANING PRODUCTS

ABRASIVES
An abrasive cleaner contains small particles of a grit substance that help cleaning products do their job. They are found in products such as toothpaste, scouring cleansers and metal polishers. When you use products containing grit substances, you need to take care that you do not damage the item you are cleaning.

ALKA SELTZER
Alka Seltzer contains citric acid and baking soda; upon contact with water the acid and base mix and fizz up (similar to the volcano trick; vinegar added to baking soda will fizz and foam over the top of the volcano).

ALUMINUM FOIL
Aluminum foil is produced by passing aluminum between metal rollers under pressure. The foil is one of the thinnest products produced and is less than 0.006 inch thick. Aluminum foil is produced from sheet coils that are heated and then passed through high-speed foil rolling mills.

Foil is shiny on only one side because as it passes through the final foil mill two thickness of foil are rolled together. The sides facing each other emerge with the dull finish, while the sides in contact with the foil mills come out shinier caused by the burnishing effect of the rollers.

Aluminum is the most commonly recycled metal in the world. Because of its ability to be easily recycled, it is considered to be enviro-friendly.

BABY OIL
Baby oil as a mineral oil base; some may contain natural herbs.

BAKING SODA
Baking soda is actually bicarbonate of soda, which is derived from the manufacture of common washing soda also, known as sal soda. Baking soda is composed carbon and oxygen molecules, which combine to form carbon dioxide gas.

All baking soda in North America is mined from the mineral Trona, found in Green River, Wyoming. The large deposit was discovered in the 1930s. Trona is actually composed of sodium bicarbonate and sodium carbonate, a very close relative. The ore is mined from deep mines, crushed, rinsed, and heated to produce sodium carbonate. The sodium carbonate is then dissolved in water and carbon dioxide is forced through the solution, releasing the sodium bicarbonate crystals. The crystals are washed, dried and packaged as baking soda.

- Baking soda will last for approximately 6 months if stored in an airtight container and in a cool, dry location.
- It can be used to neutralize acids, scrub shiny materials without scratching them, deodorize and even extinguish grease fires.
- It can be used to polish aluminum, chrome, jewelry, plastic, porcelain, silver, stainless steel and even tin.
- It can soften fabrics and remove many stains.
- It softens hard water and provides for a relaxing bath as well as an underarm deodorant and toothpaste.

BAKING POWDER
Baking powder was invented in 1849 and combines sodium bicarbonate and an acid salt to make the leavening agent. In 1854 self-rising flour was invented, which combined baking powder with flour.

Baking powder is a mixture of a number of chemicals that is used to leaven breads. The main chemicals are calcium acid phosphate, sodium aluminum sulfate or cream of tartar and sodium bicarbonate.

This mixture of acids and bases and a starch produce a chemical reaction when water is added to it to produce carbon dioxide, a gas. Since it is found in most kitchens and is a fine powder it has many other uses.

BEESWAX
Beeswax is sold in brick or chunk form and is available in most arts and craft stores or candle shops. You can also buy it directly from a beekeeper.

BORAX
Borax is a naturally occurring mineral found in evaporative deposits. Some countries use the mineral as a food additive; however, it is banned from food in the United States. It is a white powder that easily dissolves in water and is used in detergents. Use with caution and do not ingest. It is also used to neutralize the ammonia odor of urine.

- It is soluble in water, can deodorize, will inhibit the growth of mildew and mold.
- It boosts the cleaning power of soaps and detergents, removes stains and when added to a sugary substance will attract and kill insects.

CARNAUBA WAX
This is one of the hardest natural waxes and is produced from a Brazilian palm tree.

CASTILE SOAP
Castile soap is an olive oil based soap sold in health food stores and some drug stores.

CITRUS OILS (LEMONS & ORANGES)
Citrus oils are extracted from a number of different citrus fruit skins. Citrus oil may also be called "agrumen oil." It is fragrant oil that has strong solvent properties. Citrus oil contains a number of compounds such as limonene and linalool. Used as a natural cleaner and to eliminate odors.

COLA
Colas and some other sodas contain phosphoric acid as their carbonating agent. The activity of the acid can be used for a number of cleaning uses.

CLUB SODA
Because club soda contains a number of chemicals as well as the use of carbon dioxide to provide carbonation it can be an excellent cleaner. The ingredients may include carbon dioxide, carbonated water, sodium bicarbonate, sodium citrate, potassium sulfate and disodium phosphate. Some have up to 60mg of sodium per 8 ounces.

CORNMEAL
Cornmeal is a granular flour from dried yellow or white corn kernels. It has a sweet, robust flavor and commercial cornmeal is available in fine and coarse grinds. Stone-ground cornmeal is made from whole kernels and will produce a richer flour.

CORNSTARCH
Cornstarch is a derivative of corn that can be used to clean windows, polish furniture, shampoo carpets and rugs and even starch clothes.

CREAM OF TARTAR
Tartar is derived from grapes during and after the process of fermentation. Two pinkish crystalline sediments remain in wine casks after the wine has fermented; they are "argol," which collects on the sides of the cask and "lees" which collects on the bottom. These substances are actually crude tartar. The crude tartar is then de-crystallized by cooking in boiling water and allowing the remains to crystallize again.

This substance is then bleached pure white and further crystallized. As this process concludes a thin layer of very thin white crystals are formed on the surface. The name cream of tartar is derived from this thin top layer that looks like cream. It is used to produce baking powder when mixed with baking soda.

DIATOMACEOUS EARTH (FOOD GRADE)
A mineralized soil that comes from fossilized algae and sold in a powder at garden supply and nursery stores.

ESSENTIAL OILS
Essential oils are the concentrated oil of plants, which can be found in health food stores or by mail order through the Internet.

GREAT ALL-NATURAL CLEANING AIDS
While many books may recommend using these oils for different cleaning purposes, a warning needs to be added to their use. They are all-natural extracts from different plants; however, the oil is very concentrated and can actually be hazardous and should be kept away from pets and children. Once you dilute them, they are not harmful, depending on the level of dilution.

EUCALYPTUS OIL
Excellent oil for cutting grease; add a few drops to increase the grease-cutting power of natural liquid soaps when doing dishes. It works on countertops, bathtub rings and even soap scum on shower doors. It has antifungal, antibacterial and antiviral properties historically associated with the oil.

GARLIC
Garlic is grown worldwide and sold in fresh clove form or as garlic salt or powder. It is commonly used in hundreds of recipes for sauces and chicken, especially in Italian cooking. Garlic has been used as a medication for a number of illnesses throughout history. Americans consume 250 million pounds of garlic annually with a large percentage grown in Gilroy, California.

Garlic can be peeled easily by placing it in very hot water for 2-3 minutes and rinsing the garlic under hot water to loosen the skin. For a special flavor rub a clove of crushed garlic on the sides of your salad bowl before mixing your salad.

GELATIN
Gelatin can be acquired from a number of different sources; however, the most common source is animal hooves, muscle, bones and connective tissue.

Other sources include seaweed from which agar-agar is produced and Irish moss from which carregeenan is made. Both of these are popular commercial thickeners; however, carregeenan is especially useful for thickening ice cream products.

GLYCERIN
Glycerin can be found at drug stores and arts and craft stores. It is a natural solvent.

HERBS
Herbs, including cinnamon and cloves, can be used to eliminate and mask odors.

JASMINE OIL
Just a few drops of jasmine oil in an all-natural grout cleaning product is an excellent mold and mildew killer, and adds an extra whitening power.

LAVENDER OIL
Historically, lavender oil has been an excellent antifungal, antibacterial and antiviral natural oil. There is no evidence of any allergic reactions associated with the oil. It can be added to any cleaning product to provide a boost of effectiveness and pleasant aroma.

LEMON JUICE
Lemon juice, which contains citric acid, can be used as a deodorant, to clean glass, and to remove stains from aluminum, clothes and porcelain. In conjunction with sunlight lemon juice can also be effective as a mild lightener or bleach.

LEMON OIL
A few drops of this oil and odors will disappear. It can be added to any all-natural product to give an added aroma boost.

MINERAL OIL
Derived from seeds, mineral oil is found in a number of furniture polishes and floor waxes.

MURPHY OIL SOAP
Murphy Oil Soap is very popular for wood furniture, cabinets and floors; commonly sold in supermarkets.

OLIVE OIL
Not only is olive oil high in monounsaturated fat (77%), gluten-free, and contains 8 percent of your daily requirement of vitamin E in only one tablespoon, but it has amazing cleaning properties! Olive oil can be used as a polish for metal and

wood and as a cleanser for cast-iron pots and pans.

OXALIC ACID
An acid that is found in many foods, such as spinach and chocolate, oxalic acid has many cleaning uses in its pure form, but must be used with caution.

PUMICE STONE
Pumice stone is a hardened foam-like substance prepared from volcanic lava. It is very abrasive and gritty yet soft enough to be safe for a number of cleaning purposes: to remove lime buildup in toilet bowls, remove most graffiti from cement block and bricks and clean ceramic tile and even cast-iron cookware.

SADDLE SOAP
Mild soap used to clean leather as well as condition it. Saddle soap is soap with oil in it, which is why it is so good for keeping leather in good condition.

SALT (SODIUM CHLORIDE)
Salt is basically composed of two chemicals, sodium and chlorine, which individually can be very dangerous. Chlorine is a poison and sodium will actually ignite when it comes into contact with water. However, when combined, their chemical composition is altered and they become sodium chloride or as we know it, common table salt.

Because of salt's abrasive nature and absorbent abilities, it can be a very effective, inexpensive cleaning product.

While salt is an important mineral that can be beneficial to the body, in excess it may be detrimental. Body fluids and their distribution in the body depend on the location and concentrations of sodium and potassium ions. Our kidneys regulate the blood sodium levels and provide the bloodstream with the exact amount as needed.

When blood levels rise due to excess sodium ingestion, the body's thirst receptors are stimulated and fluid intake increases to balance the sodium to water ratio. The excess sodium and water is then excreted by the kidneys. When this balance cannot be maintained the result may be higher blood pressure and an increased deposition of atherosclerotic plaque material.

When salt is processed the native minerals are stripped away and it is then enriched with iodine and dextrose to stabilize it, sodium bicarbonate to keep it white, and anti-caking agents to keep it "free-flowing." Morton's Special Salt is one of the only salts that have no additives. Salt is used in almost every food that is processed and is one of the best preservatives.

STEEL WOOL PADS
To preserve the steel wool pads and avoid them rusting, just wrap the pad in aluminum foil and place it into the freezer. Placing a piece of aluminum foil under the pad if left out in a dish will retard rusting, but be sure and drain the excess water out of the dish.

THYME OIL
Add a few drops to any all-natural disinfectant product and it will boost its power. It is historically known for its antivirus, antifungal and antibacterial properties.

TOOTHPASTE
A number of toothpastes have just enough abrasiveness to be useful in a number of cleaning jobs.

TSP
Trisodium phosphate is a mixture of soda ash and phosphoric acid and is toxic if swallowed. There are a number of jobs that it can be used in place of more dangerous chemicals such as cleaning drains or removing old paint. It will not create and dangerous fumes.

VANILLA EXTRACT
Used in a number of odor-reducing products since it has the ability to linger in the air providing a pleasant aroma and masking unpleasant ones.

WASHING SODA
Washing soda is also known as sal soda, sodium carbonate or soda ash. It is a white strongly alkaline salt that is composed of transparent crystals and can be purchased in the supermarket. Washing soda can cut grease on grills, broiler pans and ovens, softens hard water and can be used as a detergent to do laundry.

WHITE VINEGAR

CAUTION:
NEVER MIX VINEGAR WITH BLEACH; THE FUMES ARE HAZARDOUS.

NATURAL PRODUCTS SHOPPING LIST

1. Baking Soda
2. Bon Ami Cleanser (has no chlorine or dyes)
3. Borax (keep away from children and pets)
4. Castile Soap (Kirk's)
5. Club Soda or Seltzer
6. Cornstarch
7. Liquid Dishwashing Cleaner
8. Essential Oils (health food store; use with caution)
9. Glycerin Soap
10. Ivory Liquid Soap
11. Laundry Detergent that states that it is perfume and dye free
12. Lemon Juice
13. Mineral Oil
14. Murphy Oil Soap
15. Pumice Stone
16. Salt (coarse)
17. Steel Wool Pads
18. TSP (use with caution)
19. Washing Soda
20. White Vinegar

AAAAA

ACOUSTICAL TILE

Purchase a professional "dry sponge" and clamp it onto a holder pole; then make passes across the tiles until the sponge gets too dirty to continue. You will then need to use another sponge. When this type of sponge gets black with dirt, it is best to discard it.

WATER LEAK STAIN
To repair a small area that has been water stained, use a small amount of white liquid shoe polish and dab it on. Hardware stores will sell a special spray paint for use on acoustical ceilings in many colors.

ADHESIVES

LEFTOVER GLUE RESIDUE
Shortening will remove glue residue from glass, metals and almost any plastic material. Smear on a small amount, wait 10-15 minutes and then gently scrub off with a scrub sponge.

AIR CONDITIONER

CLEANING OUTSIDE UNIT
Keep all dirt, leaves and debris cleared away from the outside condenser.

CLEANING INSIDE UNIT
Remove the front panel and clean out all parts that look dusty and dirty. Be sure that the unit is unplugged. Clean out the drain pan and add some baking soda to keep it smelling fresh. Do the cleaning at the beginning of every season. Keep it covered in the winter to keep some of the dirt out.

ALUMINUM

ANODIZED
This type of aluminum has a protective coating that cannot be cleaned with strong solvents or abrasives. Use a nylon-back sponge and a mild detergent and do not rub too hard or even use irregular pressure or the finish could dull.

REMOVE MINERAL DEPOSITS
You can remove mineral deposits in kettles or pans by using a solution of ½ cup of white vinegar and 1 quart of water. Bring to a boil and allow it to remain overnight. Equal parts of white vinegar and water can also be used.

ALUMINUM COOKWARE

ALUMINUM HATES HARD WATER
Aluminum cookware stains very easily, especially if you are using hard water to cook with. Certain foods, such as potatoes, will also cause the pans to stain easily. Cooking a high-acid content food such as tomatoes, onions, wine or lemon juice in aluminum will probably remove some of the stain. If a pan is already stained when the acidic foods are cooked the stain may transfer to the food and possibly turn the food a brownish color.

DISCOLORED POTS: BOIL IT OUT

Black stains on aluminum pots can be removed by boiling white vinegar in the pot up to the area of the stain. For large pots boil the vinegar in a small pot and pour it on the stain.

SHINING WITH FOODS
Cooking apples, rhubarb, lemons or tomatoes in an aluminum pot will remove stains. These foods contain just enough acid to do the job. You could also just use cream of tartar in a quart of water and boil that in the pot.

BURNED-ON FOOD REMEDY
The following ingredients will be needed:

| 1 | Tablespoon of baking soda |
| ¼ | Cup of warm tap water |

Place the warm water over the burnt area; pour the baking soda on top of the water. Allow the solution to sit for 12 hours before cleaning.

ALUMINUM SIDING

CLEANING
Remove the nozzle from a garden hose and pour in some baking soda to spray the siding clean.

APPLIANCES, KITCHEN

RUST REMOVER
A paste prepared from baking soda and water will remove rust from appliances.

GENERAL RULES FOR CLEANING SMALL APPLIANCES
➢ Be sure and unplug all appliances before cleaning.
➢ Never use abrasives since they will scratch the surface.
➢ Some small appliances need cleaning after every use, such as a can opener.
➢ Never clean an appliance until it cools down.
➢ Most small appliances cannot be immersed in water.
➢ Never take appliances apart to clean the inside unless the manufacturer's instruction tells you how to do it.
➢ Parts that can be washed should be washed in warm soapy water.
➢ Glass cleaner is one of the cleaners of choice for small appliances.
➢ Be careful of blades and sharp edges.
➢ Individual parts need to be fully dry before being reassembled.
➢ Use appliance covers to keep dust and grime out of the appliance.

CAN OPENER
To clean a can opener, try running a piece of paper towel through it.
This will pick up the grease and some of the gunk.

ARTIFICIAL HOUSE PLANTS

BLOW OFF THE DUST
Just set your hair dryer on the lowest fan setting and the lowest heat
position (cool, if possible) and blow the dust off.

A LITTLE SQUIRT WILL DO YA
To keep dust from settling on artificial house plants, just spray them
with hair spray occasionally.

ASPHALT

BLACKTOP CRACKS
It would be best to fill any crack as soon as you spot it to keep water
from getting under the slab. If the cracks are ½-inch or wider, they
should be filled with cold patch. If the crack is narrow, fill it with crack
filler. Make sure you clean out any small pieces of material before
you patch. Clean off any dust with a power washer or garden hose.

ASPHALT TILE

ONLY CERTAIN CLEANING AGENTS WILL DO
Never use any cleaner on asphalt tile that contains oils, solvents or is
a strong alkaline cleaner. Hopefully, your asphalt was sealed with an
acrylic sealer and then waxed to protect the tile. Cleaning should be
done with a mild, neutral cleaning solution and just damp mopped as
needed. Wax needs to be stripped periodically and new wax applied.
If fading occurs, you will need to purchase a restorer that can be
purchased at most janitorial supply companies.

AUTOMOTIVE

CAN PROTECTION
The lids from 1-pound coffee cans will fit a can of opened motor oil and stop the dust or debris from contaminating it.

DASHBOARD SCRATCHES
The plastic lens covering the instrument panel may get scratched, but all you have to do to hide the scratches is to wipe the plastic with a cloth dampened with baby oil.

DOOR PROTECTION
Glue an old piece of scrap carpet to the garage wall to prevent damaging the door when you open it.

REMOVING TAR
The easiest and least expensive method to remove tar is to use sodium bicarbonate on a damp cloth. However, you can also use kerosene or a special tar remover from an auto supply store. Another method is to prepare a paste of 3 parts of baking soda and 1 part of water. Apply the paste to the tar with a damp cloth and allow it to dry for 5-6 minutes before rinsing.

WINDSHIELD CLEANER
Why pay big bucks for a spray bottle of windshield cleaner? Just keep a spray bottle with white vinegar in the trunk and an old newspaper. You can clean grime and grease off the windshield as well as a bug or two.

BATTERIES

NEUTRALIZE ME
The acid around a battery post can easily be cleaned with a thick solution of baking soda and water. Allow it to soak for 10-15 minutes before washing it off. Baking soda is a mild base and will neutralize the weak acid.

TAKE 2 AND START

If cleaning the battery posts don't help when your battery is dead, just drop 2 aspirins in the battery. The acid in the aspirins will combine with the sulfuric acid in the battery and give you a quick charge.

BUMPER/GRILL

DE-BUGGING

Spraying vegetable oil on a clean car bumper and the grill before a trip will make it easy to remove the bugs when you return.

CARPETING/MATS

AUTO CARPET CLEANER

Greasy stains can be cleaned up with a solution of salt and baking soda. Lightly brush the stain and allow the powder to remain for 2-3 hours before cleaning it off.

ODOR

CAR ODORS

Place a few charcoal briquettes or an anti-static dryer sheet under one of the car seat to absorb odors.

TIRES

BLACK TIRES ARE THE BEST

It takes a lot of care to keep tires from drying out and cracking from the combination of ozone and sunlight. Tire manufactures utilize a stabilizer called a "competitive absorber." These absorbers capture the UV rays from the sun and convert them to harmless heat, which is harmlessly dissipated.

The most common of these "absorbers" is carbon black. Tires will eventually turn gray as the carbon black loses its ability to protect, thus turning the black tires gray over time. Higher quality tires have a wax compound added to the carbon black providing longer life of the tire and a slower degree of graying.

SIDEWALL CLEANER FOR TIRES

The following ingredients will be needed:

    1   Cup of baking soda (fresh)
         Cool tap water

Place the baking soda in a small bowl and add just enough water to prepare a loose paste. Wash the tires and rinse with cool water until the baking soda residue has been removed.

WASHING

ALL-NATURAL CAR WASH

The following ingredients will be needed:

    1   Gallon of tap water
    ¼   Cup of liquid soap
    8   Drops of essential orange oil

Mix all ingredients together. Wash, rinse well, then dry.

WHEELS

END THE BLACK PLAGUE

Next time you clean hubs and wheels, try spraying them with liquid oil spray. You will find it much easier to clean them next time around and much of the black carbon from the brakes will not adhere.

WINDSHIELD

AN EASY SOLUTION

If you want to keep your windshield free from frost, just mix up a solution of 1 part white vinegar to 3 parts of water and apply to the windshield. You can also just cut an onion in half and rub the fleshy area on the windshield.

CLUB SODA CLEANER

If you keep a spray bottle filled with club soda in the trunk, it will come in handy if you get bird droppings or bugs on the windshield. Even if it goes flat, it will still work great.

BBBBB

BACK PACKS

NYLON PACKS
These can be machine-washed. Be sure and close zippers and secure all straps and buckles. Always remove any stiffeners or frames from the inside before washing. Front-loading machines will do a much better and gentler washing than top loaders. Most packs have washing instruction labels with directions for cleaning.

COATED-NYLON BACK PACKS
Best if you don't machine wash a coated-nylon product; the chemical used to provide the waterproof coating will easily deteriorate if you wash it too often.

BAKING DISHES

BURNT FOODS
Heat-resistant glass dishes will burn food on very easily. To remove the burnt-on foods, warm up some liquid dish soap and let it sit in the dish for about 30-40 minutes. The burnt-on food will loosen and wash off easily.

BARBECUES

NATURAL DRIP PAN
Since you don't want to clean the fat and meat residues off the charcoal briquettes after you barbecue, you might try making a drip pan. This will also stop flare-ups. Form an aluminum pan that will be larger than the items you are cooking from two layers of aluminum foil. Cook in the pan on the barbecue and just discard after use.

IT'S MAGIC FOIL
If you barbecue on the grill, just place a sheet of aluminum foil on the grill when the coals are still very hot and it will burn off the food residues. When you use the barbecue the next time, remove the foil, crumple it up and use it to clean off the grill.

BURNER MAINTENANCE A MUST

The feeder tubes that enter the control valves located ahead of the burner should be cleaned at the beginning of every season. Spider webs and small dirt particles will clog these very easily and hamper the gas flow to the burners. It can even be a potential fire hazard. If the flames are yellowish and flow slowly, there may be a problem and a clog.

BARBECUE GRILL CLEANER

You can easily de-grease the grill on the barbecue by applying a paste of baking soda and water with a wire brush. Allow the solution to remain for 15 minutes before wiping it clean. The fire will burn away any residue that remains before you add food to the grill.

BASEMENT FLOORS

CLEANING

Floors need to be painted and sealed so that they will be easy to sweep or vacuum and won't hold the dust.

BASEMENT WALLS

MOISTURE PROBLEM

There may be a white, powdery substance on the basement walls ("efflorescence") caused by moisture that has been forced through the porous concrete by hydrostatic pressure. As the moisture evaporates it leaves a white deposit. Scrubbing with water and a brush should remove it or use a mild detergent. Best to correct the drainage problem or it will keep occurring.

BASTING BRUSHES

KEEPING BRUSHES IN TIP TOP CONDITION

Small brushes used around the kitchen, especially basting brushes, are very difficult to get clean. These brushes are usually dipped in oils and sauces and it is almost impossible to remove the stickiness.

Just wash the brushes in hot liquid soapy water, rinse well and shake dry. Place the brushes with their bristles pointing down into a cup and fill the cup with coarse salt until the bristles are covered.

The salt will draw moisture out of the bristles and keep them dry and in good condition ready for the next use. The salt is easily shaken off.

BATH MAT

RUBBER MATS
If there is a fungus among us it may be on the rubber mat. Best to soak the mat in 1 cup of borax and 10 cups of warm water for about 1-2 hours.

BATHROOM

GENERAL BATHROOM CLEANER
The following ingredients will be needed:

1	Pound of baking soda (fresh)
4	Tablespoons of liquid hand soap
1	Cup of warm tap water

Place all the ingredients in a spray bottle and shake to mix. This formula is not as harsh as one with ammonia. It is also safer around children.
- ❖ Every week, place a small handful of baking soda down the shower drain followed by some white vinegar. Wait 10 minutes and then flush with hot water.
- ❖ Unwrap fragrant soaps and leave them in a basket. This will make the bathroom smell better and will make the soap last twice as long by reducing the moisture in the bar.
- ❖ Keep a scented candle and matches in the toilet area.
- ❖ Never wallpaper a bathroom that gets easily steamed.
- ❖ Always paint using high-gloss finish paint since it cleans easily and repels soil.
- ❖ Avoid water getting on the floor by weighting down the bottom of the shower curtain.

BATHROOM MIRROR

FOG-FREE MIRROR
There are two ways to eliminate fogging up of bathroom mirrors; you can use car paste wax and place a very small amount on a cloth and wipe the mirror and buff it off with a clean cloth or you can use shaving cream to do the same job. You will be able to see yourself as soon as you get out of the steamy shower.

BATHTUB

DON'T BE HARSH
Enameled metal and fiberglass tubs can lose their luster if you use a harsh scouring cleanser or rough nylon scrub pad. Toilet bowl cleaners will also damage the finish on a tub. Use a very mild abrasive cleaner and don't rub too hard. A paste of baking soda and water should do the job. Hard water deposits will clean off using a solution of vinegar and water or straight vinegar; then flush immediately with water and dry.

RING AROUND THE TUB
The best way to eliminate the unsightly buildup of the rings that are composed of body oils, dirt, hard-water deposits and soap is to wipe the area with a washcloth when the water is going down the drain. Once it gets to be a permanent stain, it can only be cleaned with acids that will harm the finish. Vinegar and baking soda paste may do the job but you still cannot scrub with too much pressure.

BOY, AM I DISCOLORED!
Most discolorations are from hard water stains. Try covering the bathtub with paper towels that have been soaked in full strength white vinegar. Remove the towels after 2 hours and you will be amazed at the result.

BEDDING

KILL THE LITTLE BUGGERS

To get rid of dust mites, just place your bedding in a big plastic bag and place it in the freezer overnight or just wash it. To get rid of bed bugs and dust mites, place 4 dryer sheets between the mattress pad and the mattress and place duct tape sticky-side out around the entire base of the bed.

Sleep somewhere else for one night and then check the duct tape for all the dead critters.

BERRY STAINS

LEMON REMOVER

Next time you pick berries and can't get the stains off your hands, pour a small amount of lemon juice on the stained area and allow it to remain for a few minutes. The stain should just wash away.

BLACKBOARD

REMOVE CRAYON MARKS

Use a paste prepared from baking soda and water.

BLENDER

CLEANING

Fill the blender ½ full of warm water and add 1 teaspoon of baking soda and 1 drop of dishwashing detergent. Place the lid on tight. Turn on the blender briefly to prevent suds running over. Rinse.

CLEAN ME OR LOSE ME

To keep your blender and mixer working great, be sure and lubricate all moving parts with a very, light coating of mineral oil (not vegetable oil).This should be done every 3 months. Before you use a measuring cup to measure a sticky liquid, try spraying the inside with vegetable oil and the liquid will flow more freely.

BLINDS

DRYER SHEET WORKS GREAT
Airborne dust, grease and dirt accumulate on the slats of blinds and if allowed to remain for too long a period the blinds will get harder and harder to clean. Clean the blinds at least once a month before the filth gets into the plastic or wood. A lambswool duster will easily do the job. If you wipe the slats every 2-3 months with an anti-static dryer sheet the dust will not settle on the slats as easily.

BLOOD STAIN

MAKE SURE IT'S CHILLED
Bloodstains may be cleaned with club soda.

EASY REMOVAL
There are a number of ways to get rid of a bloodstain. You can sponge the area with very cold water, dry with a towel and repeat the process.

You can also rub the area with a paste of cornstarch and water or cornmeal and water. Allow it to dry (in the sun) and then brush off the residue.

BOTTLES/VASES

BOTTLE-CLEANING HINTS
> ➢ Fill the bottle or vase about 1/3 full of soapy water; add about a handful of rice (uncooked) and shake as hard as you can. This old trick still works well.
> ➢ A long-handled bottlebrush will also work, but it must be one that has bristles on the bottom and not a piece of protruding wire that can scratch the glass. A good bottlebrush can be purchased at a janitorial supply.
> ➢ Glue residue can be easily removed using vegetable oil.

BRASS

USING THE SAUCE
Brass can be cleaned using either Worcestershire sauce or ketchup.
Just pour it on and allow it to remain for a short while before wiping it
off. Rinse with clear water and dry immediately.

BRICK/CEMENT BLOCK

NO HARSH CHEMICALS
Hand scrubbing is the preferred method of cleaning brick. A wire
brush is sometimes used if the brick is really in bad shape. If you use
harsh chemicals it may affect the desired look of the brick.

BROILER PAN

ENAMEL PANS
These can be pretty stubborn at times; however, if they get really
bad, cover the bottom with a thin layer of white vinegar and place a
kitchen towel over the area. Allow it to remain for about 2-3 hours.

SUGAR AS A CLEANER
Prepare a mixture of 1 cup of white vinegar and 2 tablespoons of
sugar and pour it on the broiler pan while it is hot. Allow it to remain
until the pan cools and the pan will be easy to wash clean with hardly
any scrubbing.

BUMPER STICKERS

CUTE WHEN YOU PUT THEM ON
Bumper stickers can really be a pain to remove, especially if they
have been on for years. However, if you place the blow dryer on the
highest setting it should loosen the glue
.

DON'T HOLD THE MAYO
Mayonnaise will dissolve a bumper sticker. Just spread it on the sticker and allow it to remain for about 10 minutes before wiping it off.

CCCCC

CABINETS, KITCHEN

WOOD SURFACES
Use dishwashing soap to dampen a cloth (do not saturate the wood). Dry the cabinet with a soft clean terry cloth. Be sure and wipe dry by going with the grain or pattern (if there is one).

GREASY SHELVES
Prepare a paste of baking soda and water and spread it on the shelf; allow the paste to remain until dry before wiping off.

A STICKY SITUATION
When the cabinet drawers tend to stick it usually means that drawer gliders are out of alignment or you have debris in the tracks. They may just need to be sprayed with vegetable oil.

CAN OPENER

CLEAN WITH VINEGAR
The blade of the can opener should be cleaned using an old toothbrush and white vinegar. If you hold the toothbrush under the blade and turn the blade, all the dried food will come right off.

CANDLE WAX

ON WOOD FURNITURE
Soften the wax using a hair dryer on the hottest setting; blot up as much as you can with paper towels. Remove the balance by rubbing with a soft towel dampened in a solution of equal parts of white vinegar and warm water. Wipe the area clean with a soft cloth.

ALCOHOL TO THE RESCUE
Black soot marks on candles are unsightly and can be removed with rubbing alcohol (but not when the candle is lit!).

INTO THE FREEZER
Candle wax on tablecloths can be removed by freezing the spot with ice cubes.

CASSEROLE DISHES

BURNED ON FOOD
The way to clean burned on food from a casserole dish is to fill the dish with very hot water and add 3 dryer sheets then allow it to soak overnight. You will have an easy job cleaning the casserole the next morning. Wash with soap and water before using.

CERAMIC TILE

VINEGAR HELPS
Ceramic tile cleans up easily with just a damp cloth. It is the grout between the tiles that creates a cleaning problem. White vinegar does a very good job of getting rid of the mildew and mold that tends to take residence there.

CHINA, FINE

HAND WASH
While some china and porcelain can be placed in the dishwasher, all of it should be hand washed to be on the safe side. Be sure to place the dishes in a plastic or rubber dishpan or have a rubber mat under them. Use a mild hand dishwashing detergent and never allow the china to soak for any length of time to avoid damage to some of the colored decorations. Never pour boiling water or even scalding hot water on china. When you store china, always use separators between the dishes.

CHROME

GOOD USE FOR NEWSPAPERS
You can shine chrome fixtures by rubbing them with newspaper after the fixtures have been dampened with water. You can also rub them with baby oil and a soft cloth to clean them. Use gloves when using the newspaper so the newsprint won't get all over your hands.

CHROME & STAINLESS CLEANER
Spray white vinegar on fixtures and appliances and polish until they shine.

COFFEE MAKERS

COLD SOLUTION FOR GLASS POTS
Place 2 tablespoons of salt and just enough ice to cover the bottom of the glass pot. Add the juice of 1 lemon and throw in pieces of the lemon in quarters as well. Swirl the contents in a circular motion until you see the coffee stains disappear. The stains and coffee residues should just lift off.

CLEANING PERCOLATORS
You can remove bitterness by cleaning the percolator or other types of coffee pots by filling them with water and adding 4 tablespoons of salt; percolate or boil as usual.

AUTOMATIC DRIP MACHINES
Drip machines need their inside de-mineralized every month. The best method is to run 1 quart of white vinegar through it or purchase a product that is made for de-mineralizing. Put one or two cycles of clean water through the system before making a pot of coffee.

COFFEE STAINS

FROM CHINA CUPS
To remove coffee or tea stains from china cups rub the area with moist salt.

REMOVING BAD STAINS
A solution of equal parts of table salt and white vinegar should remove most coffee and tea stains on cups and saucers.

COMPUTERS

Computers are subject to dirt and grime being attracted to them by static electricity. The inside of the computer should only be cleaned by a technician. You can clean the outside of the computer as long as you know how to do it correctly.

CLEAN KEYBOARD
Cleaning a keyboard is a task, especially after a vacation. However, if you place a piece of aluminum foil over the keys, you won't have to clean them when you come home. A can of compressed air will clean between the keys and add a lot of life to your keyboard. Tiny mini-vacs are also sold in computer stores to clean keyboards.

CLEAN COMPUTER & PRINTER
All of the outside of the equipment can be cleaned but be sure and turn the computer off before cleaning it. Mix equal parts of white vinegar with water and then dampen a clean cloth, making sure that the cloth is only damp and never actually wet. Never use a spray bottle. Keep some cotton swabs handy for the hard-to-reach areas. An alcohol-based product from a computer store is the safest method of cleaning the housing. Smudges can be removed with denatured alcohol.

A CLEAN MOUSE IS A HEALTHY MOUSE
If your mouse has a removable tracking ball, use a 50/50 solution of white vinegar and water. Use a slightly dampened cloth that has been wrung out well and remove all visible dirt and finger marks. Use a cotton swab to clean out the inside of the ball chamber. Allow it to dry for 1-2 hours before putting it back together.

NO STATIC SCREENS
Wipe your TV or computer screen with an anti-static sheet to eliminate static electricity.

CONCRETE

NORMAL CLEANING

Wet concrete with a hose and sprinkle some laundry detergent on it; then scrub the concrete with a long-handled stiff brush. Hose it off and it should look great. Because concrete is somewhat porous it will absorb dirt and other materials very easily and should be cleaned regularly.

CLEAN OFF RUST WITH LEMONADE

Rust stains on concrete can be cleaned off by mixing up a batch of unsweetened lemonade Kool-Aid with very hot water. Just scrub the stain and it should disappear.

RUB-A-DUB-DUB

To remove grease and rust stains from a concrete floor, just sprinkle dry TSP on a wet or oily surface and allow it to remain for at least 30 minutes before washing off. You can also mix 1 part sodium citrate in 6 parts of water and add enough fuller's earth to prepare a thick paste. Spread the paste on the area that needs cleaning and allow it to remain for 5-7 days before scraping it off. Keep adding new paste if it dries out.

COOKTOPS

FAST REMOVAL

It is best to follow manufacturer's instructions for cleaning since there are differences in ceramic cooktops. All recommend that spills and foods should be cleaned up immediately before they get under a pot and cause a scratch by movement of that pot. Most can be cleaned just using a mild dish detergent and paper towel. A common cleaner is Soft Scrub. Some manufacturers recommend using a razor blade for hardened-on spills but check your instruction book first. Never use a scouring powder on ceramic cooktops!

COOKWARE (GENERAL)

SEE INDIVIDUAL TYPE FOR CLEANING INSTRUCTIONS

GREASE CUTTER
If you are expecting to have a problem with a greasy pan, try placing a few drops of ammonia in the pan with your soapsuds.

POT SCRUBBER
If you don't have a pot scrubber, just crumple up a piece of aluminum foil and scrub away.

SALT SCRUBBER
If you have a burned area, sprinkle some salt on it and allow it to remain for about 10 minutes before scrubbing the area.

PUT A LID ON IT
A fire in a pan can easily be put out by just placing a lid over the fire, thus cutting off the oxygen supply.

COOLERS, PICNIC

CLEAN THEM WELL
The plastic lining in most picnic coolers is similar to the one in your refrigerator. They need to be cleaned using a mild soapy detergent and rinsed well. If you had smelly stuff in there, it would be best to scrub it out with baking soda to remove the odor. If you are going to store it closed, leave a box of baking soda open in it. If you carried fish home in it, clean it and then use a solution of 4 parts of water to 1 part of vanilla to get rid of the smell.

COPPER

COPPER COOKWARE
Copper will not react with any food and is safe to cook in. Copper is one of the best heat conductors and is preferred by many chefs.
Copper pans, however, should only be purchased if they have a liner of tin or stainless steel; otherwise they may leach metals into the food. The tin lining must be replaced if it wears out or excess copper

may leach into the food, causing health risks. Foods that are high in acid will increase the release of copper.

"Real" copper cookware provides excellent heat distribution on the bottom as well as the sides of the pan. The copper, however, needs to be kept clean because if black carbon deposits form to any degree heat distribution will be affected significantly.

One of the worst types of cookware is the stamped stainless steel pot with a thin copper-coated bottom. The copper coating is approximately 1/50 of an inch in thickness and too thin to distribute the heat efficiently and uniformly

COPPER & BRASS
Prepare a paste of equal parts of salt and white vinegar. You can also use white vinegar and baking soda, but be sure and wait for the fizzing to subside before you use it. Rub the paste on the item with a cloth or paper towel until it is clean. Rinse with cool water and polish with a towel.

KETCHUP CLEANER
Rub ketchup on the copper bottom and allow it to sit for about 5 minutes; rinse it off with very hot water to bring back the like-new shine.

GREENS A GONER
Copper tends to tarnish to a green color due to copper oxides. To prepare a cleaning solution that really works, combine 1 tablespoon salt and 1 tablespoon flour in 1 tablespoon white vinegar. Rub this solution on the copper surface and wash with hot soapy water. Rinse and dry with a clean towel before buffing.

A SHINY BOTTOM
If you want your copper pots to look like new again, sprinkle them with baking soda and pour white vinegar over them. Allow the pots to stand for 15 minutes before rinsing. If you prefer, you can use baking soda and half a lemon to scrub them to a shiny finish. Rinse well and dry before use.

LEMON TREE, VERY PRETTY...
One of the easiest and effective methods of cleaning copper is to just use half a lemon dipped in salt. Wash, dry and buff.

COUNTER, LAMINATE

CLUB SODA CLEANING
Pour club soda on the countertop and allow it to remain for a minute or so and then wipe it up with a clean cloth. Rinse the countertop with warm water and dry it off.

COPY MACHINES

A CLEAN GLASS = CLEAN COPIES
Use a glass cleaner to clean the glass, but be careful not to saturate it and allow the moisture to fall through to the unit.

If you can't get all the small bits off, use your fingernail to loosen them. If you have some copy toner on the glass, use a small amount of nail polish remover on a tissue to remove it. That will also remove ink marks on the glass.

CLEANING THE PLATEN COVER
The underneath side of the platen cover that you close over your copy needs to be cleaned with a damp all-purpose cleaner. If the cover becomes very badly stained, it is best to replace it or the stains will show through the paper.

COPY PAPER
Remember to never handle copy paper when you have wet hands or if you have and lotion on them. This will result in poor copies and may carry on to the next job as well.

CORNINGWARE

REMOVING BURNT-ON FOODS
Place 4 parts of water and 1 part of white vinegar in the pot and bring to a gentle boil. After the water cools off try gently scrubbing the food off.

COUNTERS

INK STAINS
If you get an ink stain on the counter, try rubbing it off with baking soda and water. Baking soda and water will also remove stains from other foods such as mustard, ketchup and tea.

GENERAL CLEANING
To prepare an all-purpose cleaner for counters, mix vinegar and salt. Baking soda and water will also work well.

CRAYON

REMOVE STAINS
Moisten a toothbrush with white vinegar and rub the area lightly until the crayon is removed.

USE HAIR DRYER
Use a hair dryer set on high to melt crayon wax. Be prepared to wipe it off as it melts or you will have a bigger mess to clean up.

CRISPER DRAWER

KEEP SMELLING FRESH
After you clean the crisper bin, sprinkle a layer of baking soda on the bottom of the drawer, cover it with paper towels and repeat every 2-3 months to control odors.

CRYSTAL GLASSWARE

SPARKLING CRYSTAL
If you give your crystal a soaking in a solution of baking soda and warm water for about 5 minutes they will sparkle like new.

CRYSTAL CLEAR
If you want your crystal to sparkle, rinse them in a solution of one part white vinegar to three parts warm water.

CURTAINS

DIRT IS IN THE AIR
Airborne dirt and other particles are attracted to curtains and they need regular cleaning. Vacuuming is an excellent way of keeping them clean if done on a regular basis. If you are going to wash them, follow the manufacturer's directions to the letter or send them to the cleaners. There are also a number of companies that specialize in cleaning curtains and drapes.

LACE CURTAINS
It is best to wash lace curtains using cold water, a delicate cycle, and Woolite. If the curtains are made from cotton they have to hang dry. Polyester blends can be machine dried but only on the delicate cycle.

LINED, INSULATED CURTAINS
Insulated curtains need to be washed in cold water and line dried, then ironed on the fabric side when dry. Permanent press curtains should be washed on delicate wash and dried on delicate for the best results.

RUFFLED CURTAINS
Cotton ruffled curtains will have to be ironed and probably starched. All synthetic ruffles can be spun dry (only for a few minutes), but make sure the tiebacks are not attached.

SHEER CURTAINS
Sheers are usually made from 100% polyester. Wash them in cold water on a delicate cycle. When they come out of the washer they should be almost dry and can be hung up immediately to finish drying. Never put them in the dryer or the wrinkles will never come out.

BEATS IRONING
If you want your sheer curtains to come out of the washing machine wrinkle-free, dissolve a package of unflavored gelatin in a cup of boiling water and add it to the final rinse. The protein has a relaxing, or softening, effect on the fabric.

CUTTING BOARDS

Studies keep going on and on regarding the safety of cutting boards. Plastic cutting boards were once thought to be the best since they are less porous than wood. However, a Wisconsin Food Research Institute study reported that wooden cutting boards may be best because bacterial levels are relatively low after only a few minutes of cleaning.

If you cut any meat product clean the board thoroughly with hot soapy water immediately afterward. A study completed by the federal government's Center for Food Safety and Applied Nutrition stated that only one out of four people wash their cutting boards after cutting or preparing raw meats and poultry.

Recently, a number of companies have marketed a new cutting board that has an anti-bacterial agent imbedded into the board.

SAFE CLEANING
Avoid using chemicals to clean a cutting board. One of the best cleansers is just damp salt. Place the damp salt on a sponge or some other cleaning implement and clean away. Cutting boards also need to be disinfected after each use. To do so, use an all-natural disinfectant soap or just very hot soapy water and a soft scrub brush.

WOOD BOARDS

Any cutting surface has the potential of harboring dangerous bacteria. Cutting boards and especially butcher-block surfaces are often used to place hot pots down. When this occurs, some of the heat is transferred to the surface and into the wood where bacteria may be lurking. Bacteria like heat, which may activate them for a longer period of time or provide an area for them to survive as you prepare food. Wood boards should be oiled occasionally with mineral oil to keep them in good shape.

BUTCHER BLOCK

Butcher block will not only harbor bacteria deep down in the cracks but is also difficult to clean.

BACTERIA LOVE BUTCHER BLOCKS!

Boards need to be washed with a mild detergent, then dried thoroughly and covered with a light layer of salt to draw any moisture that may have gotten into the crevices. The wood can then be treated with a light coating of mineral oil. Make sure to use only a light coating, since mineral oil may affect the potency of a number of vitamins in fruits and vegetables.

ODOR REMOVER

Rub baking soda into the wood with a damp sponge. This should remove garlic and onion odors from the board.

DDDDD

DECALS/STICKERS

DECAL BEGONE

Transparent decals may be easily removed using a solution of lukewarm water and ¼ cup of white vinegar. Place the solution on a sponge and dampen the area thoroughly for a few minutes. If this doesn't work saturate the decal and allow it to stand for 15 minutes then soak in very hot water.

TOUGH DECALS

Paint the decal with several coats of white vinegar. Allow the vinegar to soak in 5-7 minutes before washing it off. If there is still residue allow the vinegar to remain on longer.

DECKING, WOOD

SCRUB-A-DUB-DUB

If you want to clean your wood decking, just use a mixture of 2 cups of baking soda in 1 gallon of water. It will give the deck a weathered look. Test an area first to be sure that it won't affect the finish or affect the present stain.

DEHUMIDIFIERS

CLEAN THE SWAMP POT

The water container needs to be cleaned regularly since it is a breeding ground for bacteria, mold and mildew. If you place a small amount of bleach in the water it will kill the bacteria and make cleaning easy. The tank can be cleaned out by allowing it to soak in a soapy hot water bath. Use a scrub brush and clean it out well. If you have hard water deposits left over, you will have to fill the tank with 2 parts of water to 1 part of white vinegar and allow it to remain for about 1 hour before cleaning it out.

DENTURES

SMILE!

A method of cleaning dentures that works as well as the expensive brands is to just soak them overnight in white vinegar.

DISHES

CUPS, COFFEE & TEA STAINED

Mix equal parts of salt and white vinegar and scrub the cup to remove the stains from tea and coffee.

FLOWER VASE
To remove an unsightly residue buildup from inside a flower vase or wine bottle, try using a solution of 2 tablespoons of salt, some raw rice, and 1 cup of white vinegar and shake vigorously.

MAKING DETERGENT
You can prepare your own dishwashing detergent by mixing a solution of 2 tablespoons of baking soda with 2 tablespoons of borax. Use as you would your regular dishwashing detergent.

GLASS COFFEE CARAFES
Place the juice of one fresh lemon and enough ice to cover the bottom of the carafe, add 2 tablespoons of table salt, and swirl the contents for a few seconds. The coffee stains should disappear.

REMOVE CRACKS ON CHINA
A trick used by antique dealers to remove hairline cracks on china plates or cups is to simmer the cup in milk for 45 minutes. Depending on the size of the crack the protein (casein) in the milk will fill in the crack.

DISHWASHING MACHINE

SOMETHING SMELLS FISHY
Kitchen odors are frequently found in the garbage disposal and caused by food from the dishwasher. The best way to eliminate the problem is to run the garbage disposal for a few seconds after the dishwashing cycle is complete.

GET RID OF ODORS
If you don't use your dishwasher every day, sprinkle some baking soda on the bottom to keep the odors away and allow it to remain overnight. Let it wash away when you run the next load of dishes.

TANG YOU VERY MUCH
If your dishwasher is looking dingy and has deposits on the walls, just add 1 cup of Tang to the dishwasher and run it through a cycle. It will clean the interior and refresh the inside.

WHAT A PRETTY RAINBOW, BUT IT'S ON MY GLASSES?

Spotted glasses may be caused by a lack of water flow or from hard water. If the glasses are getting a rainbow hue then it is probably from using too much detergent. This can also be caused by water not being hot enough. Try running the sink faucet until hot water starts running out! Also, opening the dishwasher too soon after it has finished will cause this problem.

DISINFECTANT

HERBAL DISINFECTANT

The following ingredients will be needed:

1	Teaspoon of essential rosemary oil
1	Teaspoon of essential lavender oil
1	Teaspoon of essential lemon oil
1	Teaspoon of essential eucalyptus oil
½	Teaspoon of essential peppermint oil
½	Teaspoon of essential rose oil
1/8	Teaspoon of essential love bud oil
2 ½	Ounces of fresh distilled water

Place all the ingredients in a medium bowl and mix thoroughly. Store the solution in a well-sealed glass jar. Place a small amount in a spray bottle and keep in the bathroom to freshen it up.

GERM ALERT! CALL OUT THE HEAVY ARTILLERY

Germs love moisture. If you keep surfaces dry it will reduce the incidence of bacteria getting a foothold and causing odors and unhealthy conditions. Disinfectants will kill bacteria and almost all molds, but only for a short period of time. Therefore it is necessary to

49

clean the surfaces that are more susceptible to contamination more frequently than most other area of your home.

SIMPLE HOUSEHOLD PINE DISINFECTANT
The following ingredients will be needed:

2	Tablespoons of borax
2	Cups of very hot tap water
¼	Cup of pure lemon juice
6	Drops of pine essential oil

Place all the ingredients into a spray bottle and shake until well blended. This will be as effective as most standard brands.

DOORS

WOODEN DOORS
Wooden doors usually sealed up well or have a number of coats of paint on them. They can be cleaned with a cloth or sponge dipped in an all-purpose cleaner. Never wash doors in the sunlight since they will streak.

DRAINS

PREVENTION
To prevent a drain clogging up, pour ¼ cup of salt down the drain, followed by boiling water. In fact, just pouring boiling water down a drain once a week will help to keep the drain clear.

THE UNCLOGGER
Pour ¼ cup of baking soda down the drain followed by ½ cup of white vinegar to unclog most drains. Let the solution sit for about 2-4 minutes and pour at least a quart of boiling water down the drain to flush it all out. Be sure not to allow the mixture to remain in the drain for more than a few minutes, especially if you have plastic pipes.

FIZZ, FIZZ
Drop 3-4 Alka-Seltzer tablets down the drain, then pour in a bottle of white vinegar. After 3-5 minutes run hot water down the drain.

POP, POP INSTEAD OF FIZZ, FIZZ

Cola contains phosphoric acid in enough of a concentration to clean out a clogged drain in many instances. In an emergency, just pour at least 3 cans of cola down the drain and wait for about an hour before flushing with boiling water.

DRINKING GLASSES

PRYING THEM APART

Sometimes it is hard to get drinking glasses apart. When this occurs, put a few drops of vegetable oil along the side and wait 2 minutes; they should come apart easily.

DRIVEWAYS (ALSO SEE CONCRETE OR ASPHALT)

HERE KITTY, KITTY

If you have a driveway that has oil residue that is hard to remove, cover the area with sand or cat litter and allow it to remain for 2-3 days before sweeping it off.

DRYERS

VACUUM TO THE RESCUE

Lint and dirt can collect on the exhaust panel on the inside of the dryer and around the burners on gas dryers.

This is a fire hazard and these parts need to be cleaned by a professional about every 2-3 years. Also vacuum the rear area of the dryer and as far inside as you can reach safely.

IMPORTANT NEWS YOU CAN USE

Dryer sheets have caused many dryers to either burn out the heating unit or cause a fire by blocking the filter.

Even though you clean out the lint filter every time you use the dryer, there is a buildup of residue from the dryer sheet that sticks to the mesh and cannot be seen. The coating is invisible to the naked eye.

Try running water through the mesh filter. If the water will not go through easily it may be partially or completely blocked and you will see the problem for yourself. Use an old toothbrush every 3 months to clean the screen and you will see the difference. This will lower your electric bill, make the dryer more efficient and protect your property.

DUSTING

MONEY SAVER
Don't bother buying fancy dust cloths that are treated to attract dust when all you have to do is to dip a piece of cheesecloth in a mixture of 2 cups of water and ¼ cup of lemon oil. Allow the cheesecloth to air dry and it will do just as good as the expensive cloth.

FEATHER DUSTERS
These are capable of removing dust around knickknacks and artificial plants, but tend to redistribute the dirt. The feathers just tend to flick some of the dirt around in the air.

LAMBSWOOL DUSTER
A lambswool duster relies on the natural oils in the wool as well as static electricity to attract and hold the dust particles. A lambswool duster is better than a cloth and excellent for dusting uneven and intricate objects. It is best to use a smooth action and not clean hurriedly from one spot to another. The only drawback is the small tufts of wool that you may leave on an object that protrudes.

A LITTLE OF THIS & A LITTLE OF THAT
You can make your own dusting oil by mixing three parts of light mineral oil mixed with one part of corn oil and adding one drop of lemon or clove oil.

EEEEE

EGG STAINS

FROM SILVERWARE
Wash immediately in hot soapy water and dry immediately.

FROM STAINLESS STEEL & TIN
Remove excess by scraping up all the excess with a dull knife. Wash the area with a cloth dipped in warm soapy water.

FROM MASONARY TILE
Wash excess and then wash the area with a solution of washing soda and water (never use soap) with a soft-bristled brush. Rinse thoroughly with water.

FROM SYNTHETIC FUR
Scrape as much of the egg from the surface as possible. Prepare a solution of dishwashing detergent in hot water and make suds. Use a cloth and dip it into the suds. Clean the area gently and then wipe with a clean cloth.

FROM LEATHER
Gently, scrape the excess off the leather. Prepare a solution of a mild soap and warm water and mix into suds. Use the suds only on a sponge to clean the area then dry with a clean cloth.

If you still have a greasy-looking area, try some cornmeal to absorb the grease. Leave the cornmeal on for a while to allow it to absorb the grease before brushing it off gently.

CLEANING EGG MESSES
If you pour salt over the top of a broken egg mess it will make it easier to clean up.

ON AUTOS
1. Do not allow eggs to remain on the car overnight if possible.
2. Remove any shell pieces that are not dried onto the car.
3. Wipe up as much of the egg as you can with a soft towel trying not to scratch the paint with any eggshell.
4. Soak a towel in a solution prepared from 50/50 warm water and white vinegar.
5. Place the saturated towel on the area and allow it to remain for 20 minutes.
6. Remove the towel and wipe away any remnants. Dry with a soft towel.

ENAMEL PANS

TOUGH TO CLEAN
Soak the enamel pan overnight in salt water. The next day, boil salt water in the pan for a few minutes. The stain should come right off.

ERASER

CLEANING PENCIL ERASER
Pencil erasers need to be cleaned off occasionally or they do more damage than good. Rub them lightly with a clean emery board to clean them.

EXHAUST FAN

RANGE HOODS
Remove the grease filter and soak in a degreaser solution using an all-purpose cleaner. Streaming hot water will also do the job and scrubbing with a brush helps. Aluminum filters can be placed in the dishwasher, but not with the dishes.

Be sure that the filter is 100% dry before reinstalling it. Vacuum up in the unit with the filter removed as best as possible to get rid of the dust. If it looks greasy do not vacuum the area before you clean out the grease or you will clog the hose on the vacuum.

BE GENTLE NOW
Light bulbs in vents need to be removed and very gently cleaned with cool water and soap.

EYEGLASSES

CLEANER
Prepare a solution of 5 drops of white vinegar in 2 tablespoons of water and place it in a small spray bottle. Use the spray on the lenses to do a great job of cleaning them.

HEAD FOR THE WASHROOM
Anti-static dryer sheets make excellent eyeglass cleaners and will even prevent them from fogging up. You can also use a coffee filter to clean lenses.

FFFFF

FABRIC SOFTENER

VINEGAR SOFTENER
Add 1 cup of white vinegar to the rinse cycle of every wash load. This can be done for baby clothes or any other clothes from family members who are allergic to fabric softener. If you add the vinegar during the last rinse, it will also eliminate static cling.

MAKING YOUR OWN DRYER FABRIC SOFTENER
The following ingredients will be needed:

½	Cup of baking soda (fresh)
1	Tablespoon of cornstarch
1	Tablespoon of arrowroot powder
2	Drops of essential rose oil (optional)

Place all the ingredients into a small bowl and mix well. Place a small amount in a small cloth bag that can be well secured with a drawstring. Tie or place it into the dryer with the load. Be sure the bag is well sealed or it becomes a bit messy.

FABRICS, GENERAL

ACETATE
Acetate is a general all around fabric used in clothing, linings, draperies, upholstery fabrics, as a fill for quilts and mattress pads. It is stain and mildew resistant. However, it will fade and will do better if dry-cleaned. Check the label for cleaning instructions. Always press on the wrong side and use a low heat setting. Acetate is easily damaged by acetone, alcohol and acetic acid. Do not allow the fabric to be in sunlight for too long a period or it will be damaged.

ACRYLIC
Acrylic can be found in many types of clothing, especially sweaters, pile fabrics, blankets, robes and draperies. It is very stain and mildew resistant and will maintain colors well. Acrylic can be machine-washed and dried on low heat setting. Acrylic sweaters should be blocked for the best results. The light and white colors can tolerate chlorine bleach if necessary. If ironing, use only the low heat setting since the fabric is heat sensitive. Carpeting will show crushed traffic lanes and the indentations from furniture will be permanent.

COTTON
This is a natural plant fiber that can be found in linens, curtains and clothing or blended with polyester to make permanent press fabrics. It is colorfast and is comfortable to wear as well as being long wearing. Polyester and cotton can be laundered in hot water and will take scrubbing without damage. Whites and colors should be washed separately. Be sure to follow manufacturers' directions.

Never use vinegar or an acid spot remover on the fabric. You can use a hot iron. If you turn the item inside out when washing you can reduce the lint that is released. Cotton is best washed in warm water and dried on the permanent press setting.

LINEN
This is a natural plant fiber that is comfortable in hot climates. It is used in blouses, summer suits, dresses and linens.

Linen resists staining better than cotton and is moth-resistant; however, it does tend to wrinkle easily. The more you wash it the softer it will become and it washes best in hot water. Be sure and press the cloth with a hot iron while it is still damp. Linen is sensitive to acids.

NYLON
A very popular fabric used in carpeting, clothing, sporting goods, hose and furnishings. It is long-wearing and very strong as well as resistant to abrasions, mildew, stains and insect damage. It is best to use a fabric softener and wash whites and colors separately. Use the medium dryer setting for the best results. Nylon attracts oily stains and develops static cling. Whites will yellow in sunlight and chlorine bleach. Use a warm iron as needed.

POLYESTER
This is a blend of cotton, rayon and wool and can be used in almost any type of garment. Commonly used in permanent press and as a fiberfill for pillows, carpeting, jackets and sleeping bags. It is strong and very colorfast and will resist wrinkling, abrasion, mildew, moths, sunlight, perspiration and stretching. Should be washed in warm water and dried at medium heat using fabric softener. Do not leave in dryer and iron on permanent press setting if necessary. It will attract oily stains and develops static cling.

SILK
This is a natural fiber used for clothing, linens, handkerchiefs and scarves. It has a very luxurious look, resists wrinkling and soiling but can easily be damaged by many chemicals and some foods. Silk usually must be dry-cleaned; however, some silks can be hand-

washed (check the label for cleaning instructions). If you do press the garment, be sure and press on the wrong side with a warm iron while it is still damp. Silk is sensitive to acids and chlorine bleach and may be stained by perspiration and exposure to sunlight.

SPANDEX
This is an elasticized fabric that is used for foundation garments, swimwear, sportswear and support hose. It is resistant to stains, body oils and perspiration. Spandex fabrics can be machine washed and dried on a low heat setting; however, some may require dry cleaning if other fibers are blended with it. Chlorine bleach will damage the fabric; if ironing, be sure and use the lowest heat setting and keep the iron moving.

WOOL
Natural animal fiber used in clothing, blankets and carpeting. It is wrinkle-resistant, does not lose color easily and is naturally water-repellant. Does have the potential for shrinkage and should be dry-cleaned. Check the label; some wool garments can be safely hand washed or machine washed on delicate with Woolite. Be sure to block the garment and air dry. Woolens can be damaged by moths, chlorine bleach and strong alkaline cleaners.

FAUCETS

SHINE 'EM UP
Keep a dryer sheet under the sink in the bathroom to clean and shine the faucets.

CLEANING WATER DEPOSITS
Chrome or brass is easily cleaned with all-purpose cleaners; however, hard water scale buildup on the faucets can cause a bit of work. Using a mild acid will solve the problem. If the buildup is in hard to reach places, spray white vinegar in the area. Vinegar will usually break down these deposits very effectively. Use a small plastic putty knife to loosen the deposit. Be sure and rinse the area well and don't allow the vinegar to remain on the chrome or brass fixture for any length of time.

FIBERGLASS

NATURAL FIBERGLASS CLEANER
The following ingredients will be needed:
- 1   Cup of borax or baking soda
- ¼   Cup of white vinegar

Place the borax or baking soda in a small bowl and add the vinegar until the powder is good and damp. Sponge the solution on the area that needs cleaning and rub until clean. Sponge off with warm water; then rinse well.

FILES

PESKY WOOD SHAVINGS
Cleaning wood shavings from workbench files, nail files and rasps can be a real pain. By using a piece of masking tape to cover the length of the tool and pressing it firmly, you can pull off all the shavings or nail debris.

FILTERS

AIR CONDITIONER FILTERS
Washable air conditioner filters should be cleaned once a month during the months they are being used. Vacuum off as much dirt as you can. Wash the filters in a solution of 1½ tablespoons of baking soda to 1 quart of water. Do not replace the filters before they are 100% dry.

FIREPLACE

FOILED AGAIN
To easily clean your fireplace place a double layer of aluminum foil on the bottom of the fireplace and remove it after the ashes have cooled. Fold it up and throw it away. If you do this every time you make a fire it will be much easier to care for the firebox.

A LITTLE SQUIRT WILL DO YA
When you are cleaning the ashes out from the grate, use a spray bottle on a fine spray to keep the ashes down before you sweep them out. This will keep the ashes from flying around the room.

THE CURE FOR A DISCOLORED FIREPLACE
If your bricks are getting discolored by smoke and soot, just clean them with a spray-on oven cleaner.

GENERAL RULES FOR CLEANING THE FIREBOX
> ➢ Since most fireboxes are made from metal the hot ashes will eventually burn through and ruin the box. The fewer ashes that are in the box, the more heat you will get, so clean it often.
> ➢ Never clean out the box if there is the slightest chance that there is a hot coal in it. Best to wait if you are not 100% sure.
> ➢ Be sure and open the damper as wide as possible, allow all the fine dust to go up the chimney and not in the house or in your lungs.
> ➢ Set the container to hold the ashes as close to the opening as possible. Metal buckets are recommended for this job; line it with a plastic bag.
> ➢ Go slowly and scoop up the ashes with a small dustpan. Gently lay the ashes into the container; don't dump them. You need to get rid of the bulk of the ashes, not every last bit.
> ➢ Be sure and seal up the plastic bag before trying to move the container or you may spray ashes all over the room.
> ➢ Use the ashes for fertilizer in the garden or add to a compost pile.

CLEAN BRICK OR STONE
Dip a brush in white vinegar and scrub the area; then immediately use a damp towel or sponge to wipe the excess moisture off the area. Do not leave vinegar on the brick; be sure and rinse the area with clean water and dry.

I CAN HELP, DON'T THROW ME OUT
Don't dispose of all the ashes. A good fire needs a two-inch carpet of ash under the grate. This will help the fire start faster and help to radiate heat into the room.

FIREPLACE GLASS

REMOVING SMOKE STAINS

Prepare a solution of 1 cup of white vinegar in 1 gallon of warm water and place the solution in a sprayer. Spray on the glass, allow it to remain for a few seconds and then rinse it off with a cloth dipped in warm water. Dry thoroughly.

FLOCK OR FOIL WALL COVERINGS

CAREFUL CLEANING REQUIRED!

Wipe the dirty area with a dry sponge. If that does not work, try wringing out a cloth dipped in all-purpose cleaner (make sure it is almost dry) and very gently wipe the surface of the flock. With foil, use a dry sponge or very cautious damp wiping. If you have to use a small amount of water, be sure and dry it off immediately. Rub lightly to avoid streaks.

FLOORS, GENERAL CLEANING

NO-WAX FLOOR CLEANER

The following ingredients will be needed:

1	Cup of white vinegar
¼	Cup of washing soda
1	Tablespoon of Castile soap (liquid)
2	Gallons of very hot tap water

Place all the ingredients into a bucket, blend well, and mop the floor as usual. This formula will eliminate any greasy condition.

FLORESCENT LIGHTS

COUGH, COUGH
When fluorescent lights seem to getting darker it usually means that the bulbs have not been cleaned and dusted regularly.

FLOWERS, ARTIFICIAL

SILK
Craft shops sell containers of compressed air that will blow the dust and dirt off silk flowers and do so safely.

Be sure and follow the directions. If you place a hair dryer on low, it will accomplish the same task.

A small paintbrush or feather duster can also be used with excellent success. If you have big leaves, try using an electrostatic dust cloth. If you need to wash off the flowers, dip or wash each one individually with cool Woolite solution.

PLASTIC
These flowers need weekly dusting with a feather or lambswool duster. They can also be sprayed with hairspray occasionally, which will keep the dust from settling. If you keep the plants in the kitchen, they will eventually acquire a film of grime and need to be cleaned with a mild detergent. Fill a bucket or the sink with the solution and if the plant can be inverted, just swish it under the water solution for a few seconds to loosen the grime and wipe the leaves or flowers.

CLEANS ALL KINDS
Place the flowers in a plastic bag and add $\frac{1}{4}$ cup of table salt; shake the bag gently. The flowers should come out bright and clean.

FLOWERS, SILK

ATTRACTIVE SALT
Cleaning silk flowers is easy if you place them in a plastic bag with 2 tablespoons of salt and shake vigorously while holding on to the stems. Salt tends to attract the dust.

FORMICA COUNTERS

SHOULD YOU EVEN BUY A FORMICA COUNTERTOP?
There are number of disadvantages in buying a Formica countertop: abrasive cleaners will scratch and dull the surface, sharp knives will leave scratch marks and a hot pot will actually melt the finish.

Also, warping can occur if the area is wet for too long a period. The seams are too easily seen depending on the quality, some will even fade in time.

MILD BLEACH
When a Formica countertop gets stained, one of the best methods of removing the stains is to bleach them out with lemon juice. Just spray the juice on and allow it to remain on the area for about 30-40 minutes before scrubbing the area with baking soda. Rinse with clear water and dry.

SCRATCH REMOVER
Some stains and scratches can be removed from Formica counters by using a paste prepared from baking soda and water.

FURNACES

DIRTY FILTER = DIRTY HOME
You can spend less time cleaning and dusting if you change your filters regularly. Duct cleaning is also important and should be done by a professional. The cost is usually from $75-$300 depending on the size of the home. It is also a must if someone has allergies.

STEAM BOILER
You may have rust and scale in the boiler which will constrict the passages and lower the efficiency. The boiler will need to be flushed. There may also be a buildup on the heating surfaces of soot from combustion; however, this job is for a professional.

VACUUM, VACUUM
Remove vent covers that are easy to remove and vacuum inside as best you can, using a crevice tool. The more dust and dirt you can keep out of the furnace, the more efficient it will run. Do not vacuum around a pilot light or the light may go out from the suction or the exhaust.

FURNITURE

LEATHER RESIDUES
Most leather tabletops can be cleaned using a soft cloth dipped in ¼ cup of white vinegar mixed with ½ cup of water. Dry immediately with a clean towel.

REVIVING LEATHER LUSTER
Mix equal parts of white vinegar and boiled linseed oil, place in a spray bottle, shake well and spray. Spread evenly using a soft cloth and wait a few minutes before rubbing the solution off with a clean cloth.

GLASS-TOP FURNITURE
One of the easiest methods of cleaning glass is to lightly dampen a cloth with white vinegar. This will clean off all the fingerprints and smudges.

PROTECTING THE WOOD FINISH
If you run out of wood oil, try using mayonnaise. A very light coating rubbed into the wood will help protect the finish. It should be rubbed in well; be sure not to leave a residue.

Leftover tea can be used on wood furniture and also to clean varnished furniture.

WATER RINGS ON WOOD

When you place a glass with a wet bottom on wood furniture the water may react with the stain in the wood or whatever wax was used and leave a white ring. These rings may be removed by mixing a small amount of salt with 2 tablespoons of vegetable oil. Apply the solution and allow it to stand for at least 1 hour before rubbing the area gently. Baking soda may be substituted for salt if a less abrasive mixture is desired for more delicate surfaces.

Another method is to prepare a solution of equal parts of white vinegar and olive oil and apply with a soft cloth moving with the grain of the wood. Use another clean, soft cloth to polish.

WATER STAIN REMOVER

The following ingredients will be needed:

1	Ounce of toothpaste (not gel)
½	Teaspoon of baking powder

Place the ingredients into a small bowl and mix well. The mixture will be a little gritty, which is OK. Gently rub the area and allow the mixture to remain until it is dry before gently buffing it off and placing a coat of furniture polish on the area.

A NUTTY, WOOD SCRATCH SOLUTION

The broken edges of nuts can be rubbed gently on wood furniture to mask scratches. Just find a nut that matches the color and the results will surprise you. The most common ones are pecans, walnuts and hazelnuts.

POLISH OR WAX BUILDUP REMOVER

Prepare a mixture of equal parts of white vinegar and water, dip a cloth in, squeeze out very well and move with the grain to clean off polish and wax residues.

UPHOLSTERED FURNITURE

LOOK FOR THE LABEL INFORMATION

"w"	**Means safe to clean with water**
"S"	**Means use dry cleaning solvent only**
"WS"	**Means that either method is OK**
"X"	**Means clean by vacuuming or lightly brush**

If there is no label then proceed with shampooing only after you test an inconspicuous area for colorfastness. Be sure and vacuum first.

DRY CLEANER FOR UPHOLSTERED FURNITURE

The following ingredients will be needed:

1	Cup of baking soda (fresh)
1	Cup of cornstarch

Place the ingredients into a sifter and sift into a small bowl. Mix the powder with enough cool water to prepare a loose paste. Sponge on the fabric and allow it to stand for 20-30 minutes to dry before brushing off or vacuuming.

GGGGG

GALVANIZED METAL

CLEAN BEFORE PAINTING

Galvanized metal should be primed before painting and should be cleaned with white vinegar. Allow the metal to completely dry before painting and the paint will go on much easier. Also, you won't have to touch it up as frequently.

GARAGE ROLL-UP DOORS

ROLLERS DO NOT OPERATE SMOOTHLY

Make sure that the rollers are not damaged; if they are replace them. If they are clogged with grease and grit, they should be removed and cleaned in a solvent solution such as mineral spirits and then reinstalled.

GARBAGE DISPOSAL

The disposal works by using a small motor which powers a flywheel that throws the garbage into a shredder, producing a pulp that will easily flush down the drain.

There are two major types of garbage disposal units: the batch feed, activated by turning a stopper and the continuous feed, operated by turning on a wall switch.

CLEANING A DISPOSAL
You can actually clean out the garbage disposal by pouring ½ cup of salt down into the disposal and running the water as you activate the disposal.

RUBBER GASKET
Be sure and clean both sides of the rubber gasket since this is one cause of odors in the disposal. Some gaskets can be removed; however, most are stationary.

LEMON FRESH & CLEAN
To clean a garbage disposal and keep it clean and smelling fresh, try grinding up lemon peelings the next time you use lemons. You can also place some baking soda in the disposal and allow it to remain for 20 minutes before washing it down.

SAFE ODOR REMOVAL
Never place any type of chemical drain cleaner into a garbage disposal. If you need to get rid of odors use a small amount of white vinegar.

SEASONING THE DISPOSAL
Just pour ½ cup of table salt in the garbage disposal and run water as usual. This will clean and freshen up the disposal. However, if you prefer you could pour ½ cup of baking soda in the drain and flush it with very hot water.

GARDEN TOOLS

SAVE THOSE HANDLES

Wood handles need to be treated occasionally with boiled linseed oil. Use a clean cloth and rub the oil on the handle.

A CLEAN TOOL IS A HEALTHY TOOL

All tools should be wiped clean after every use or eventually they will rust and deteriorate. Most garden tools have a protective coating, which will wear away over time. Acids in the soil and fertilizers will eat away at the coating.

GLASS

REMOVING DRIED PAINT

Heat some white vinegar and place it on the painted areas on the glass. This will soften the paint enough that it will scrape off easily with a single edge razor blade.

GLASS COOKWARE

CLEANING GLASS

Use a white nylon scrub pad or soak the dish in hot soapy water to loosen the particles. Baking soda is a mild cleanser that can be used on glass cookware. Never use steel wool or a harsh scouring cleanser or you will scratch the surface.

NO-SCRUB SOLUTION

Fill the stained glass cookware with water and add 6-7 Alka-Seltzer tablets and allow it to soak for 1-2 hours. The stains should easily clean away without any scrubbing.

GLUE

GRANITE COUNTERS

CLEAN THEM PROPERLY

- Blot stains immediately or they may penetrate the surface.
- To clean the surface use soapstone available in hardware stores or use mild soap and water.
- Always use a soft clean cloth and never an abrasive pad or steel wool.
- For stains, combine 2 tablespoons of dishwasher soap and water into a thick paste. Place the solution on the stain and cover it with a piece of plastic wrap. Allow it to stand overnight.
- If the stain is oil-based (grease, milk, etc.) make the paste from hydrogen peroxide instead of the dishwasher soap.
- Acetone will remove ink stains from granite.
- For non-oil stains, use pure bleach made into a paste; allow the paste to remain for 30 minutes and rinse.

SPIT SHINE?

If you would like a quick shine on your countertop, just wipe it down with white vinegar.

GRASS STAINS

THE GREEN, GREEN, GRASS OF HOME

Grass stains will be easily removed with toothpaste; scrub the toothpaste into the material with a toothbrush before washing. Another method is to rub the stain with molasses, allow it to stand overnight, and wash with regular dish soap. If all else fails, try methyl alcohol, but be sure the color is set. Try an area that won't show first.

GRATERS

GREAT GRATER TIP
Cleaning the grater will never be a problem if you use a small piece of raw potato before trying to wash it out. Sometimes a toothbrush comes in handy, too.

SOAK IT!
If you don't have time to clean a dirty grater, the next best thing is to just drop it into a tub of soapy water. It will be easy to clean when you have the time.

GREASE

KITCHEN GREASE STAINS
Grease stains can be removed from most kitchen counters by wiping them down with a solution prepared from equal parts of white vinegar and water.

ON KITCHEN WALLS
If you accidentally get grease on the wall, place some cornstarch on a cloth and rub it into the grease stain until it is gone.

ON PAPER OR PAGES
Grease stains on paper or book pages are permanent and cannot be removed. You can, however, stop the grease stain from getting any worse by placing clear cellophane tape over the grease stain on both sides of the page or paper.

ON HANDS
Car grease can be removed from your hands by mixing 1 teaspoon of olive oil with 1 teaspoon of salt and rubbing it into the grease. Do this for about 3 minutes before you wash it off.

GRIDDLE

CLEANING STICKY MESSES
If you rub a griddle with a small bag of salt it will stop food from
sticking and prevent smoking. If you sprinkle salt on a freshly washed
griddle or waffle iron and then heat it in a warm oven and dust it with
salt, food will not be able to stick the next time you use it.

COOL IT!
All griddles, even non-stick ones, should always be allowed to cool
before being placed in hot soapy water and cleaned. Some griddles
need to be re-seasoned after a period of time and a number of
cleanings. It is best to check the manufacturer's instructions to keep it
in top shape.

GROUT

KILLING MOLD & ELIMINATING MILDEW
Mold loves to grow and multiply in warm, damp places and the grout
around tile is just the location for them. Cleaners that will kill the mold
can easily be prepared and commercial preparations are not really
necessary. The best tool to use on grout when cleaning is an old
toothbrush that is not too stiff. If the brush is too stiff it will remove a
small amount of the grout every time you clean it and eventually you
will have to re-grout.

STUBBORN STAINS
If abrasives will not remove a stain on grout, try using a folded up
piece of sandpaper. Be sure to not scratch the tile when doing this.

GUM

FLAKE IT OFF
The best method of removing chewing gum is to use ice and just
flake the gum off.

VINEGAR TO THE RESCUE
You can remove chewing gum from most fabrics, carpeting and upholstery by placing some white vinegar on the gum and allowing it to remain for about 10 minutes. The gum should loosen up and be easy to remove. However, be sure that the item you are using the vinegar on is colorfast. You may want to try a hidden area first to be on the safe side.

GUTTERS

BE FIRM WITH YOUR GUTTERS
If you need to clean your gutters, try using an old fan belt. It has excellent flexibility, and is firm enough to do the job without scrapping the paint off.

HHHHH

HANDBAGS

LEATHER BAGS
It is best to clean leather with saddle soap and cream leather cleaner. These should be available at any shoe repair shop. If the bag is patent leather, which scratches easily, use a patent leather cleaner on a soft, damp cloth.

FABRIC BAGS
For any type of fabric material bags use Woolite and warm water but don't saturate. After rinsing using a damp cloth, let the bag air dry.

STRAW BAGS
Vacuum to remove any dust or dirt that gets trapped between the straw strands. The bag can be cleaned using a mild hand liquid cleaner for dishwashing liquid on a damp cloth. Hang it up to dry but not in the sunlight or you may end up with a smaller bag.

SUEDE BAGS
Use a suede brush to remove any debris. However, the only way to clean a really dirty suede bag is to have it professionally done. Check with your dry cleaner or shoe repair store for the service.

HOUSEPLANTS

CLEANING
Shine up the leaves by wiping them with a solution of ½ cup of white vinegar in 1 gallon of cool water.

IIIII

ICE, ON SIDEWALK

ICE REMOVER
You won't need cat litter or rock salt; just use baking soda to de-ice the steps or walkway. Baking soda will provide traction and will melt away the ice. It is safe and will not harm the outside surfaces, shoes or any indoor surfaces if you track it inside. You can mix it with sand for even better traction.

INK

POCKET STAIN
If possible, it is best to handle this problem while the ink is still wet. Use a small amount of salt and pour it on the stain then dab it and be careful not to spread it while you clean the area.

INKA-DINKA-DOO
Ballpoint ink stains on the wall can be removed using full-strength white vinegar on a sponge. Repeat until all of the mark is gone. Stains from ballpoint pens can also be removed with hair spray or milk.

STAIN THAT HAS SET
If the stain has set on a white fabric, just put cold water on the fabric and apply a paste of cream of tartar and lemon juice. Allow it to stand for 1 hour before washing as usual.

IRON

CLEANING
When starch builds up on your iron causing it to stick,
run the hot iron over a piece of aluminum foil to clean it off.

A SHOCKING SOLUTION
A pipe cleaner dipped in white vinegar should be used to clean the
holes in the iron after it is completely cool. Make sure it is unplugged.

DIRTY BOTTOM
If the bottom of the iron gets dirty, clean it with a steel wool soap pad.
If you want to make it shiny again, run a piece of waxed paper over it.

JJJJJ

JEANS

JEAN SMARTS
Blue jeans should only be washed in cold water and placed in the
dryer for only 10 minutes on medium heat. Shake out, smooth, and
hang the jeans on a wooden hanger to continue drying.

REMOVE STIFFNESS
Next time you wash your jeans or even if they are a new pair and you
want to eliminate the stiffness, just add ½ cup salt to the water when
you add the detergent.

KKKKK

KITCHEN SINK

SINK ODORS
Odors in the sink can usually be eliminated by running very hot water
down the drain or placing 2 tablespoons of baking soda in the drain
and allowing it to remain for a few minutes before running the hot
water. If this fails place 1 cup of white vinegar in the drain and allow it
to remain for 20 minutes before flushing with hot water.

STEEL SINK RUST REMOVER
Prepare a thick paste of baking soda and warm water and allow it to remain on the stained area for about 2 hours. Buff the entire sink with the paste using a damp, soft cloth and rinse with cool water.

UNDER SINK ODOR
If you keep a box of baking soda under the kitchen sink, it will eliminate the musty odor.

BAD STAIN SOLUTION
Prepare a paste of 1 cup of borax and ¼ cup of lemon juice. This can clean heavy stains and sometimes even a rust stain by placing some of the paste on a sponge and rubbing it into the stain. Rinse with warm water.

LLLLL

LACE

YUK
Lace doilies should be hand washed in sour milk for the best results.

OLD LACE
Grandma's lace needs to very gently hand washed in warm water and Woolite. If there are any metal fasteners they will need to be removed and sewn back on later or they may rust and ruin the lace. Allow to air dry and gently squeeze the water out--never wring it out. Never use chlorine bleach or any other harsh chemicals.

LAMPSHADES

SHADES
Weekly vacuuming is the best way to preserve a nice lampshade. If it has intricate designs, use a soft vacuum dust brush and reduce the suction to its lowest point.

DUST MAGNETS
Heat and light from lamps will draw dust, grease, insects and other airborne dirt into the shade. The material in lampshades tends to hold onto the material and that makes them very hard to clean. Unless you have an expensive shade, it may be best to just replace the shade every few years. Vacuuming helps, but may still not make them look great.

LAWN FURNITURE

RESIN FURNITURE
Since you cannot use abrasives on resin furniture you need to clean the furniture with baking soda on a damp sponge and then rinse.

LEATHER

Saddle soap is not really a cleaner, but just provides the softness by forcing oils into the leather. The item to be saddle soaped should be as clean as possible before using the saddle soap or the soap has the tendency to force dirt back into the leather.

LEATHER REVIVAL
If you want to revive the beauty of leather try beating two egg whites lightly, then applying the mixture to the leather with a soft sponge. Allow it to remain on for 3-5 minutes before cleaning off with a soft cloth, just dampened with clear warm water. Dry immediately and buff off any residues.

LEATHER FURNITURE

POLISH LEATHER FURNITURE
Boil 2 cups of linseed oil for 1 minute and allow it to cool before stirring in 1 cup of white vinegar. Apply with a soft cloth, allow it to stand for 1-2 minutes and then rub off gently.

LINOLEUM

BE GENTLE, OR LINOLEUM WILL HAVE A CRACK-UP

Linoleum can be manufactured by using a mixture of resins, small particles of cork or wood fibers and linseed oil that is adhered to a canvas, burlap or felt backing using high pressure. Never use a strong alkali-based cleaner on linoleum since they tend to ruin the linseed oil binder and may cause the floor to develop cracks, thus shortening the usable life of the flooring. Best to use a mild detergent solution and dry as soon as has been cleaned. A linoleum formula should never be used on a wood or cork floor.

BE GONE, DULL, GREASY FILM

Mop the floors with 1 cup white vinegar mixed in 2 gallons of warm water. This will remove dull greasy film. Polish with club soda.

DON'T USE RUBBER BACKING!

Never use a foam or rubber-backed mat or rug on a linoleum floor or it will cause permanent discoloration.

LIPSTICK

A SLIPPERY SUBJECT

Lipstick stains will clean out of clothes by using Vaseline. You can also rub the area with shortening and then wash in sal soda.

MMMMM

MAHOGANY

REMOVE WHITE SPOTS

Cover the spots with petroleum jelly and allow it to remain for 2 days before cleaning it off.

MAKEUP

YUMMY
If you accidentally spill a small amount of makeup on your clothing, don't try and wipe it off with a cloth or you may smear it. Try using a piece of fresh white bread.

MARBLE

MARBLE, THE TOUGHEST OF THE TOUGH, BUT BE GENTLE!
Marble is one of the toughest floor surfaces. Marble is basically naturally compressed, crystallized limestone, that can range from somewhat porous to very compact. It can be polished to a high shine and will remain that way with very little care almost forever. The solutions mentioned below will clean and keep marble shining with a minimum of effort. Strong detergents and abrasives should never be used on marble since they will dull the shine and may cause deterioration of the marble.

MY TOP ISN'T SHINY ANYMORE
If your marble top has lost some luster it may be caused by dust. Try wetting the marble well and then washing it with a mild detergent, using a soft brush. A marble cleaner and polish is available at most hardware stores.

You can also wet the marble surface and sprinkle it with a marble-polishing powder. Rub it in and then polish with a clean cloth. Putty powder (tin oxide) is recommended.

MICROWAVE OVEN

NEATNESS COUNTS
If you don't clean up the microwave regularly the spills will cook onto the surface. To remove them easily, place a sponge dipped in water or a small dish with ½ cup of water in the microwave and cook on high for about 2 minutes; then wipe up.

HARDENED GUNK
To clean out hardened gunk, place a cup with about 4 ounces of water in it and run the microwave for a few minutes. Keep the door closed and allow it to remain for another few minutes and loosen up the dried food on the walls should be loosened. Never use metal scrapers or abrasives in the microwave.

LEMON CLEANER
If you have food that has hardened inside the microwave oven, prepare a mixture of 3 tablespoons of lemon juice and 1½ cups of water and place it into a microwave-safe bowl. Cook on high for 8 minutes and allow the steam to condense inside before wiping off the crud.

MILDEW

DEW TELL
White vinegar will remove mildew and mildew stains safely without needing to air out the room. It will remove mildew from shower curtains, fixtures, furniture and most painted surfaces. You can dilute the vinegar with water if the mildew is not too bad or use it full strength if it very bad. You can also mist-spray white vinegar on the back of carpets to prevent mildew from forming.

MIRRORS

SEEING THE LIGHT
Mirrors can be brightened by rubbing them with a cloth dampened with alcohol. Alcohol will remove a thin film of oil that is left from cleaning agents.

STOP FOGGING UP
Place a thin coating of non-gel toothpaste on the mirror and wipe it off with a damp cloth.

SHINE 'EM UP
Make a pot of strong tea and allow it to cool off completely. Dampen a cloth in the tea, wipe the mirror, and then buff with a cloth.

NNNNN

NO-WAX FLOORS

SHORT-TERM SHINE

Even no-wax floors will eventually lose a lot of their shine without some waxing. Over time, the glossy layer will wear away and need waxing. The only way you can keep a no-wax floor from ever needing waxing is to wear socks and have no children! Foot traffic will eventually take its toll.

OOOOO

OIL SPILLS

YUK!

When you spill oil on the kitchen floor it can be quite a mess to clean up. Next time it happens, sprinkle a thick layer of flour on the area and wait a few minutes for the flour to absorb the oil. Use a dustpan and broom to clean up the flour and then spray the area with a degreaser window cleaner. Wipe up the balance with paper towels.

MOTOR OIL CLEANUP

The following ingredients will be needed:

1   Bag of non-deodorized kitty litter
2   Cups of washing soda

Spread the kitty litter on the oil spill and rub it into the oil to absorb it. Brush up the kitty litter and place more kitty litter on the spill. Repeat the process until all the oil is gone. The balance of the residue can be cleaned by brushing with the washing soda and a small amount of water.

OVENS

USE A TEFLON LINER

Hardware stores are now carrying Teflon oven liners that are great for the bottom of the oven. If you have trouble finding one check the Internet. They are easy to locate and worth the price.

SALT MAKES CLEANING EASY

Keep a small container of salt near the oven or at least in a cabinet where you can get to easily. As soon as an oven spill occurs, pour a small amount of salt on the spill. The spill will not adhere to the oven and will be easy to remove.

GLASS OVEN DOOR

Dip a wet sponge into baking soda to clean a glass oven door.

CLEANING OVEN RESIDUE

After you clean the oven there always seems to be some residue left over. To remove the residue, spray a 50/50 solution of water and white vinegar in the oven and wipe off. This will also eliminate the smoking when you turn the oven on the next time you go to use it.

PPPPP

PAINT BRUSHES

SOFTENING HARD BRUSHES

Place the brush in hot vinegar until the bristles become soft. If that doesn't work, boil them in vinegar.

HOW SOFT I AM

After you clean a paintbrush, rub a few drops of vegetable oil into the bristles to keep them soft.

PANELING

REAL OR IMITATION WOOD

Cleaning paneling is not too hard as long as the paneling has a protective coating, which is usually varnish. If it does have a finish, use Murphy Oil Soap from a hardware store. Apply the soap sparingly and clean from the top down. Dry and buff with a clean, dry cloth. Harsh cleaners will remove the finish and eventually ruin the paneling.

PEWTER

BE GENTLE
Pewter is a soft metal that you need to be gentle with when cleaning it. To clean, add some flour to a mixture of 1 teaspoon of salt and 1 cup of white vinegar until you can prepare a smooth paste. Apply the paste with a soft cloth and allow it to dry for about 30 minutes before rinsing with warm water. Be sure and remove all paste residue from the small grooves.

REMOVE CORROSION
You can remove corrosion from pewter by just gently rubbing with 0000# (superfine grade) steel wool dipped in vegetable oil.

PLASTIC CONTAINERS

ONE OF THE BEST CLEANERS
Prepare a paste of baking soda and water, place it on a sponge, and clean out plastic bowls or other plastic containers. Baking soda is the best plastic container cleaner since it cleans and deodorizes as well.

HOW RED I AM...
Anytime you place a food that contains tomato sauce into a clear plastic container, the container will pick up some of the red color and you may never get it out. The acid in the tomato assists the color in getting into the matrix of the plastic. To avoid discoloration rub some vegetable oil on the inside of the container with a piece of paper towel before adding any tomato product. Another method, which sometimes works, is to soak the container in cold water for 4-6 minutes before adding the tomato product.

PORCELAIN

IT'S THE "REAL" THING
Real porcelain bathroom fixtures can be cleaned with almost any cleaner with the exception of abrasive ones, which may scratch the surface.

Acid de-scalers will not hurt the surface. However, delicate porcelain figurines need to be hand washed using a mild hand detergent and should never be placed in a dishwasher.

PORCELAIN CLEANED LIKE NEW
Water marks can be removed from porcelain sinks and tubs without scratching the surface and ruining the finish. Mix a gentle scouring powder prepared from 1 cup of table salt and 1 cup of baking soda. Place some of the mixture on a sponge and it should do the job.

POTS & PANS, GENERAL

BAKED-ON FOODS
To clean baked-on foods after using a pan, place a dryer sheet in the pan and add water. Allow the sheet to remain overnight and you should be able to sponge it clean the next day. The soapy agent in the sheet will loosen the dried-on foods.

QQQQQ

QUILTS

INCLUDES COMFORTERS
The majority of quilts and comforters are machine washable, but to be sure check the label before washing them. If you are not sure just how safe it is to wash them, take them to the dry cleaners.

RRRRR

RANGE TOP

CLEANING STOVETOP BURNERS
Those little vents in your stovetop burner need cleaning out occasionally. One of the best ways is to use pipe cleaners and just

poke them through a few times to clean out any debris that has found a home in there.

NEVER CLEAN THESE WITH A HARSH CLEANER
The burner top is usually aluminum and should never be cleaned with an oven cleaner. With any type of oven cleaner, however, make sure that there is good ventilation or the lining of your mouth and throat could be chemically burned.

BURNER PROTECTION

Next time you brown meat or pan fry on the stovetop, try placing inverted aluminum pie plates over the burners to protect them from the splattering grease. The pie tins can easily be cleaned and reused.

REFRIGERATORS

REFRIGERATOR TOPS
After you clean the top of the refrigerator, place overlapping sheets of plastic wrap on top. When it gets dirty, just remove a layer and replace it with a clean one.

BE GENTLE NOW
The inside of refrigerators have easily scratched surfaces and a harsh abrasive cannot be used. Mix a solution of club soda with 2 tablespoons of salt to clean out the spills and eliminate any odors.

A CLEAN COIL IS A HEALTHY COIL
If you clean the coils underneath or on the back of the refrigerator you will have substantial energy savings. Purchase an inexpensive condenser cleaning brush and be sure to clean the front plate. The backing, which is usually cardboard, is very important to the running of the refrigerator; it keeps air being pulled over the hot condenser and thus keeps it cool. If this cover is gone the compressor will eventually burn out.

RUST (GENERAL)

BYCYCLE HANDLEBAR RUST

Prepare a paste from 6 tablespoons of salt and 2 tablespoons of lemon juice and apply the paste to the rusted area using a clean dry cloth. Rub vigorously, rinse off and dry.

COLA WORKS GREAT TOO

If you're having a problem with a rusty nut or bolt, try placing a few drops of ammonia or hydrogen peroxide on it for 30 minutes.

SSSSS

SAP

BUTTER SAP REMOVER

Next time you get sap on your hands and can't get it off, just put some butter on your hands, rub lightly and wash it off.

MAYO SAP REMOVER

To remove sap or tar, spread a thin layer of mayonnaise on the area and allow it to remain for 5-7 minutes before wiping it off. One application usually works.

SCISSORS

CLEANING BLADES
When scissor blades get gummed up and dirty, never use water to clean them or the fasteners that hold them together may get rusty. Wipe the blades with a clean cloth dipped in white vinegar and dry them with a towel.

SCORCH

THAT BURNING SENSATION
A scorch can be removed by rubbing a raw onion on the scorched area and allowing the onion juice to soak in thoroughly for at least 2-3 hours before washing.

NO ONE WILL EVER KNOW
If you scorch a garment, try removing the scorch with cloth that has been dampened with vinegar. Only use a warm iron, not too hot.

THIS IS CORNY
Next time you scorch a white shirt, wet the area and pour some cornstarch on it. Allow the area to completely dry before brushing it off.

SCUFF MARKS

BORROW A PENCIL
If you want one of the easiest ways to get rid of black scuff marks on the kitchen floor, just use a pencil eraser.

SEPTIC SYSTEM

THERE'S A STRANGE SMELL COMING FROM THE BATHROOM
If you have a septic tank, you are probably familiar with an occasional strange smell and know to have the tank pumped or to add special

bacteria. However, if you are not on a septic tank and you smell a strange odor, it may be from sewer gas, which contains methane. The odor is usually associated with sulfur and you should call your gas company or a plumber as soon as possible. Plumbers have special gas detectors and can locate the problem and correct it.

SHOWER DOOR

STOP SCUM BUILDUP
To avoid soap scum buildup on shower doors, clean the door with baby oil once a week.

CLEANING
Clean the shower doors with a dryer sheet to remove soap scum.

SHOWERHEAD

COUGH, COUGH, I'M ALL CLOGGED UP
If the showerhead is clogged with hard water deposits, you will need to remove the head and soak it in white vinegar overnight. If the holes are clogged badly, you may need to use a strong piece of thin wire and push it through each hole.

SILVERWARE

POTATO WATER
There is a starch in potatoes that is released into the water when you boil potatoes. Save the water and place your tarnished silverware in it, and allow the silverware to remain for at least an hour before removing and washing off.

BAKING SODA TARNISH REMOVER
To remove tarnish from silverware, sprinkle baking soda on a damp cloth and rub it on the silverware until the tarnish is gone. Rinse well and dry.

SKUNK SMELL

TOMATO JUICE REMEDY--FOR PETS

Use 100% tomato juice and place it on the area that smells. You can sponge the juice on the pet's face as long as you don't get it in their eyes. Allow the acid from the tomato juice to neutralize the odor for about 4-5 minutes before washing it off. Shampoo and mildly scrub the pet. If the smell is not gone, repeat the next day.

VINEGAR TO THE RESCUE

Prepare a solution of 50/50 white vinegar and water and bathe your pet in it, rinse with water, and repeat using less vinegar if possible. Be careful not to get the vinegar in the pet's eyes.

FROM CLOTHING

Soak clothing in a solution of 1 cup of white vinegar in 1 gallon of water. Allow the clothes to remain in the water overnight for the best results.

SLIDING DOORS

MAKES FOR EASY CLOSING & OPENING

The tracks on a sliding door are a settling location for almost anything that will fit into the space: bug bits, hair, toy parts, food particles, dust and dead foliage. They need regular vacuuming and cleaning or all that grit will wear down the plastic wheels and you will end up replacing them. Most all-purpose cleaners will do the job and spraying a small amount of oil in the track will help keep things rolling easily.

You will need a small bristle brush or even a toothbrush to clean all the small crevices. The door can be removed for easier cleaning, but have someone do it who knows how to get it back on.

The track should also be cleaned using a cup of white vinegar in a bucket of soapy water. Scrub the track well and use a toothbrush to get into the small cracks if necessary.

STAINLESS STEEL

WORKS GREAT!
To clean stainless steel, apply a light mist of full-strength white vinegar and buff with a soft cloth.

SUEDE

CONDITIONING GARMENTS
If you want to clean and condition a suede item, wipe it with a soft cloth that has been slightly dampened with white vinegar.

TTTTT

TAR

USE ONLY THE UNSALTED
Butter or margarine will remove tar from clothing; just rub until it's gone. The butter is easily removed with any type of spray and wash product.

TEAPOTS

REMOVE LIME RESIDUE
Coffeepots, teakettles are notorious for hard water residue buildup. When they get really bad, fill them with white vinegar and run them through a cycle or boil the vinegar in them and allow it to remain overnight.

TOILETS

BROWN-OUT

Brown stains can be unsightly in the toilet bowl. The best way to remove them is with cola. Just pour 2 cups of cola into the toilet bowl and swish it around; close the lid and allow it to remain overnight. You should be able to just flush and the brown stain will be gone. Borax on a toilet brush will also do the job.

CLEAN TOILETS WITH ALKA SELTZER
Just drop 2-3 Alka Seltzer tablets in your toilet and wait 20 minutes before scrubbing with a toilet brush. The citric acid and the bubbles will work great.

TOOLS

RUST PREVENTION
If you place a few mothballs, a piece of chalk, or a piece of charcoal in your toolbox you will never have any rust on the tools.

UUUUU

URINE, PET

BAD PET!
After you blot it up and clean the area with hot soapy water and rinse it well, try cleaning the area with 1/3 cup white vinegar in 2/3 cups of water. Dab on the vinegar solution, then rinse well.

USE CLUB SODA
Blot up as much urine as possible and pour a small amount over the stained area and blot again. Club soda will eliminate the stain.

VVVVV

VASES

BROWN FLOWER STAINS
Use a wet paste prepared from salt and a small amount of water to scrub the stains from the inside of a vase.

The stains usually come from leaving flowers in the vase for too long a period. If you can't reach the area, prepare a very strong salt solution and shake vigorously.

NARROW NECKERS
When you have residue that is stuck to the bottom of a vase and you don't have a bottlebrush, just bubble the problem away by filling the vase half full and adding 3 Alka-Seltzer tablets. As soon as the fizzing stops, place your hand over the top, shake it up, then empty it.

VINYL, FLOORS

YELLOW HERE, YELLOW THERE

Yellowing is usually caused by moisture or a rubber-backed mat. Rubber-backed mats and many padded area rugs should not be used in an area that may have a moisture problem. Many of these mats and rugs have a petroleum-base and the stain will never come out.

FOOD STAINS, BEGONE!
To remove coffee or fruit juice stains from a vinyl floor, mix 1 part of glycerin in 3 parts of tap water. Soak a kitchen towel in the mixture and place it over the stain overnight. Wash the area thoroughly in the morning. You can also use household bleach, which works great on food stains.

WWWWW

WAFFLE IRON

CLEANING STICKY MESSES
If you rub a griddle with a small bag of salt it will stop food from sticking and prevent smoking. If you sprinkle salt on a freshly washed griddle or waffle iron and then heat it in a warm oven and dust it with salt, food will not be able to stick the next time you use it.

GRID CLEANING
The areas between the grids tend to accumulate grease and are very hard to get clean. One of the best methods is to place a vinegar soaked paper towel between them and let it sit overnight then use steel wool to clean. If you have a non-stick surface, follow the manufacturer's instructions for cleaning.

WALLPAPER

CLEANING WASHABLE WALLPAPER
Washable wallpaper is paper with a plastic coating and can be cleaned using minimal water on a clean cloth or sponge. Use the water very sparingly and never saturate the paper.

- **Grease Stain:** Hold several layers of white paper towels over the spot and press with a warm iron until the grease is absorbed.
- **Crayon Stain:** You have to remove grease, wax and color with a crayon stain. Try and first scrape off any excess with a dull butter knife, and then use a warm iron and the same method for grease stains. *Best to buy washable crayons for kids.*

CLEANING SCRUBBABLE WALLPAPER

These scrubbable papers are made from vinyl or special vinyl-impregnated paper and can be scrubbed with a foam cleaner or all-purpose detergent. Be sure and use a soft cloth or a sponge and rinse well. Never use any abrasive cleaners or you will scratch the finish. Scrubbable wallpaper is good for kids' rooms or rooms that will get a lot of use.

CLEANING FABRIC WALLPAPER

If they are vinyl-coated they will be easy to clean with a sponge dampened in soapy water. If they are burlap or grass cloth, best to go by the manufacturer's suggestions.

CLEANING VINYL WALLPAPER

Never use an abrasive cleaner, even a soft-scrub type. Also, never use any type of solvent cleaner or it will dissolve the ink. Use a mild dishwasher detergent and water for the best results.

WALLS

DON'T BE A PAINT REMOVER

While spots may be easily cleaned from most wall surfaces, remember that depending on the type of paint you used, you may be repainting the area you are going to clean. Depending on the type of stain and the type of paint, they may be incorporated into one another if the stain has been on the wall for too long a period. Wall stains should be removed as soon as possible once you notice them. Careful, as doesn't take very much rubbing to remove the paint with the stain.

WATER RINGS

REMOVING WATER RINGS

Mix vinegar and olive oil in a one-to-one ratio and apply with a soft cloth using slight pressure in a circular motion. See the section on Furniture for further information.

WINDOW PANES

STREAKER
If the sun is shining on your windows, try not to wash them until they are in the shade. When they dry too fast they tend to show streaks.

ON A CLEAR DAY
Mix up a solution of ½ cup of white vinegar in 1 quart of warm water and use it to clean the windows. You can also use a solution of 1-2 tablespoons of lemon juice in 1 quart of water.

NEWSPAPER CLEANER
Prepare a solution of 50/50 white vinegar and water and dip an old black and white newspaper in the solution. Clean the glass with the damp newspaper until the glass is almost dry, then shine the window pane with a piece of dry newspaper or a cloth. This really works well!

FROST-FREE
To eliminate the cleaning of frosted-up windows in a cold climate, rub the inside of the windows with a sponge that has been dipped in a solution of saltwater. The windows will never frost up again!

WINE STAINS

CARPETS
Sop up all you can and then sprinkle salt or baking soda on the area immediately after the spill. Allow it to remain for an hour before vacuuming it up. Do not vacuum up wet liquid unless you have a shop vacuum that will handle it.

WOOD, GENERAL

CLEANING PAINTED WOOD
Prepare a solution of 1 teaspoon of washing soda in 1 gallon of hot water. Wash with a dampened cloth and rinse dry immediately.

WOOD FLOORS

BLACK HEEL MARKS
To remove black rubber marks on wood floors, try using lemon juice or a superfine steel wool pad and rub very lightly with the solvent-based wax you would ordinarily use.

WROUGHT IRON

PROTECT MY IRON
Liquid wax will protect wrought iron and help to retard rusting. Never use liquid wax on wrought iron fireplace accessories since it may catch fire.

A RUSTY PROBLEM
Remove the rust stains with kerosene and a fine grade of steel wool. If it does not come off easily, allow it to remain on for a while to loosen the rust.

YYYYY

YELLOWING

REVIVER
When clothes become yellow, they can be revived and the original color or whiteness brought back by soaking them in a solution of 12 parts of water to 1 part of white vinegar. Allow the item to remain in the solution overnight and wash as usual the next day.